Talking about Bereavement

Rosamond Richardson

An OPTIMA book

First published in 1980 by
Open Books Publishing Ltd

This edition published in 1991 by
Macdonald Optima, a division of
Macdonald & Co. (Publishers) Ltd

A member of Maxwell Macmillan Publishing Corporation

British Library Cataloguing in Publication Data

Richardson, Rosamund
 Talking about bereavement.
 I. Title
 306.9

 ISBN 0-356-20236-4

Macdonald & Co. (Publishers) Ltd
165 Great Dover Street
London SE1 4YA

Typeset in Times by Leaper & Gard Ltd, Bristol

Printed and bound in Great Britain by
The Guernsey Press Co. Ltd, Guernsey, Channel Islands

CONTENTS

Give sorrow words: the grief that does not speak
Whispers the o'erfraught heart, and bids it break.
Shakespeare: *Macbeth*

Writer and broadcaster Rosamond Richardson originally trained in art and design at St Martin's School of Art, London. She has written numerous books on the country-side: *Seasonal Pleasures*, *Country Harvest*, *Discovering Hedgerows* (to tie in with a BBC series of the same name which she co-presented) and *Swanbrooke Down* as well as several cookery books, including Sainsbury's bestselling *Vegetarian Meals*. Rosamund Richardson lives in East Anglia and is a regular contributor to BBC Radio Cambridgeshire.

Acknowledgements

My sincere thanks to Dr Gwyneth Young of the Brook Hospital, Lewisham; Mr Christopher Boothby of the West Suffolk Hospital, Bury St Edmund's, Suffolk; Mr Donald Morrison of Colchester Maternity Hospital, Essex; Mr David Morris of Wimpole Street; Dr Emanuel Lewis of the Tavistock Clinic, Hampstead; Dr Thelma Bates of St Thomas's Hospital, London; Aileen Walker-Smith of the Camden Bereavement Centre, London; to Erica Griffiths, Jane de Selincourt and Jane Bird. I am indebted to the tape typists who transcribed the tapes of the interviews so ably and efficiently. Permission to quote from 'Krishnamurti's Notebook' on page xxi is acknowledged with thanks to the Krishnamurti Trust Limited, Brockwood Park, Bramdean, Hampshire SO24 0LQ.

Above all, my heartfelt thanks to all the people who so willingly and openly talked to me, without whom this book could never have been put together.

Author's Note

This book is a collection of conversations with people who have been bereaved, describing their feelings of grief and relating their experience of loss in their own words. The stories speak for themselves: they cover a wide spectrum of loss, from stillbirth through neo-natal death, the loss of children of various ages, to the death of a spouse or parent. Too little is talked about death, bereavement and grief in our society, and we have forgotten the skills of handling them properly. They are subjects that need to be aired.

Bereaved people often feel isolated and rejected by the silence that they may encounter during a time when they most need support and understanding – in the form of a listening ear. Owing to a combination of fear and ignorance, understanding and sympathy are not always forthcoming from those who are at hand to help, and the bereaved are left alone and uncomforted. Too little is generally known about the patterns and conditions of grief, and the taboos that surround the subject of death in our hygienic and mobile society encourage us to turn away from it and 'get on with life'. There are some supports that the medical profession and voluntary organisations offer (see page 184), but they are less than adequate to cover the field, and often the mourner is too overcome by his own grief to seek them out. Perhaps if a book were at hand he could turn to that.

This is not a book with a message: there is no one answer to the problems and mysteries involved. In any case, the variety of losses, and reactions to them, are legion, and no one book could encompass them.

Mystery surrounds the subject of death and grief, and mysteries are frightening: we prefer to look the other way at things we *do* know about. If we can't talk to each other about them, then we can at least read about them and perhaps learn something from the story of someone else's experience. Whether or not we have been bereaved ourselves, we may possibly gain some insight into what is, after all, so very much a part of everyday life.

Rosamond Richardson

Introduction

Malcolm: Dispute it like a man.
Macduff: I shall do so;
But I must also feel it as a man.
I cannot but remember such things were
That were most precious to me.

Shakespeare: Macbeth

No one loss is the same as another, and no loss is reparable: nobody is ever the same after losing someone they love. Loss entails change: it causes a change in our expectations, and the grief that follows it is partly the pain of relinquishing past expectations: grief is the price we pay for love, attachment and hope. No one person's reaction to loss is the same as another's, however similar the loss may appear: comparisons are meaningless since the spectrum of loss is so wide and human beings so various. The pain of grief, however, is universal, and many of the experiences surrounding death and bereavement are common to all who go through them.

Gain is the creed of today's society and we do not like to look loss in the face and examine it: we prefer to sweep it under the carpet and count it as a kind of failure. But the open confrontation of the loss of a loved one, and of the grief that follows it, can be an enriching experience and an education in the diversity of human behaviour.

In our society, expectations are geared to life and living, not death and dying, so we are not comfortable with the idea of death, grief and bereavement. Longevity is commoner than it used to be and people often do not experience a close bereavement until they are comparatively mature. We are not familiar with the process of dying and the management of death, because so many deaths occur in hospital: a dead body, a wake, an undertaker, a funeral, are all outside our general experience, whereas 100 years ago they were a part of everyday life.

Most of us are frightened of death: we fear the unknown. Even though the unknown cannot be known, if we were more familiar with dying people we might no longer have the same fears. For most people the concept of death is associated with skeletons, corpses, darkness and pain, so we protect ourselves with a sense of the unreality of death which is encouraged by our over-exposure to it in the media: so much 'news' is about death that we imagine ourselves to be immune from it. Fear of the consequences of death are also common, both to the dying and to the bereft: fear of loss, of change, of carrying unknown burdens, of loneliness, of separation from someone we love.

Fear of death in the abstract is one thing, fear of dying another. Frequently a dying person is not frightened of death itself, he is frightened of pain, of becoming ugly, of losing control over his actions; he is frightened by his fears and fearful of talking about them. He is frightened of separation from the people he loves and the world he knows. Yet it could be said that it is easier to die than to survive: for the dying person, suffering ends with his death, but begins or continues for his family.

There are many kinds of bereavement. There are obvious differences between loss by accidental or sudden death, and the reaction to the death of a person who is known to be dying: grief at sudden death is often, although not always, more severe and lasting. A third type of bereavement is encountered when a child dies: in that instance the attachment is of a special nature and particularly strong. A parent-child relationship is a unique one and among its primary ingredients are expectation and hope for the future. The love of a parent for a child is perhaps the deepest in the human experience of love: the degree of closeness to the child makes the loss a very damaging one.

Divorce is another kind of bereavement, although I have not attempted to cover it in this book. It is loss of a particularly painful kind because it involves all the negatives: failure, hurt, guilt, unforgiveness and bitterness. Many divorcees suffer symptoms of grief, and are often as badly damaged as they would be by a death. Breakdown of marriage is the death of love, whereas after the death of a person the love-bond continues in the memory. Love has gone but the subject is still there, and the victims are left in the hold of the worst elements in their nature: anger, frustration, remorse, bitterness and guilt, all of which cause deep damage and distress. Many of the people I have talked to about death have said that, however sad their own loss, they thought divorce must be worse to live through.

Socially, and particularly within a predominantly unspiritual society, the subjects of death and mourning are still taboo: like most taboos this is the product of fear. The danger of any taboo subject is that it runs the risk of becoming pornographic: there exists a covert fascination about dying, death and grief. The idea of becoming voyeurs of the dying and bereaved is repulsive. What we need is an open approach which will lead to understanding and compassion for the dying and bereaved, as well as an ability to face our own death. Let it be said also that a sense of humour is needed too. With our inability to face death and talk about it has gone our ability to laugh about it. It is essential to retain a sense of humour and keep the whole thing in proportion. There is too much that is grey, heavy and lugubrious about our attitude to death: it could do with the leaven of laughter.

Our fear of death decrees that we tend either to ignore our mourners or else to treat them with bluff good cheer. The belief in the virtue of the stiff upper lip is indomitable. We tell them to cheer up; or we point out that someone else is worse off than they are; or we compare their loss to a similar one; or, worst of all, tell them to snap out of it. The family doctor will more often than not sedate them with fashionable tranquillizers. It is the worst possible approach: the overriding need in most bereaved people is simply to talk about their loss. They need a shoulder, arms, a good hug, a listening ear. Not advice: there is very little advice that is helpful, nor are they seeking it. To say 'I *do* understand' effectively puts a stop to their flow, and the last thing they are interested in is a comparison of someone else's situation: bereavement, being the selfish condition that it by nature is, leaves the mourner interested exclusively in his or her loss. Sedation will merely suppress or postpone its symptoms and problems.

Too seldom will a friend or neighbour have the insight to stop and just be there; to offer themselves as that long-term listening ear, to sit patiently and listen whenever required. It is relatively easy to help at the onset of grief, and many people do rally round: it is later on that consistent support is needed. A newly-bereaved person is in a state of shock and feels numb and unreal – even euphoric – in the period immediately following death. It is when the natural anaesthetics have worn off and the pain starts that they need help. The role of a friend or neighbour is vitally important in a mobile society where the family is often scattered and where people have not always got the roots they used to have in the community. By expressing his fears and emotions, and by sharing his grief, the mourner can arrive at an acceptance of his loss. All the people interviewed for this book expressed relief and gratitude at the chance to talk uninhibitedly and at length about their loss.

People must be given permission to grieve; we should not be embarrassed at the display of tears, distress or despair; or at the expression of fears and feelings. They are part of a natural behaviour pattern, more readily recognised in the past and in other societies. The dying should also be allowed to grieve and to share their emotions with those who are caring for them: to share grief then can be as valuable to them as to those who they will leave behind. The bereaved, however, should be given permission to *stop* grieving also, once they have, as it were, done their duty to the dead: too often society disapproves of the person who has 'picked up their pieces' within whatever time span, and has the courage to face life again with confidence. There are no rules about how long it will take and it is uncharitable to assume the recovery from loss is a form of betrayal. It is, after all, from *not* accepting change that pain, and damage, are caused: eventual acceptance of loss depends on what sort of people we are and on the circumstances of the loss.

The attitude of the medical profession to death and bereavement is complex, and often criticised. There is no doubt that the system as it stands fails more often than not in the care of the dying and bereaved. Since so many deaths nowadays are 'institutionalised' deaths in hospitals the issue is an important one. Hospitals are not in general geared to the care of the dying. For most doctors death is a daily event and signals the end of their responsibility. All too often the bereaved are given a sad bag of possessions and left to find their bewildered and confused way home, to face alone the mystifying bureaucratic processes of death certificates and registration. Too seldom is follow-up care offered to them. A doctor's training does not normally include care for the dying or for the bereaved. In view of this, and considering the heavy workload of all doctors, our expectations of them in these areas are unrealistic. Like anyone else, a doctor has fears and emotions aroused by the dying patient, but has neither the time nor the capacity to express and share them. As a professional it is not really expected that he should, nor would the strain be possible for him as a human being. An impossible change of gear would be demanded of him, to switch between the care of the dying person, his own private grief at the death, handling the bereaved relatives and then turning to the beds where he is curing patients. His training is geared to prolonging life, not to the problems of death and dying.

Although those in the best position to help the bereaved are people who have had similar experiences themselves or are specially trained, doubtless by training doctors in the symptomatology of grief, a deeper understanding on their part would make it possible for them to give better care. GPs especially should be educated in the needs of the bereaved, which extend far beyond the prescription of pills, because it is often the GP to whom a distressed person will turn. Primarily, however, it seems that there is a major role here for the social worker, or bereavement counsellor, who can be involved with the dying and their family at home or in hospital, and then can offer follow-up care while it is needed. There is, after all, a preventive aspect to bereavement counselling, since emotional problems left unsolved can lead to physical and medical ones. Terminal care support teams, which provide care for the terminally ill and follow-up bereavement care for their families, have been set up in London at St Thomas's Hospital and the Royal Marsden, and also in Edinburgh. Local council projects are springing up, like the Camden Bereavement Centre (071-833 4138) in London which offers domiciliary bereavement counselling by trained volunteers, and educational programees for young people in the field of bereavement. There are many voluntary organisations (see page 184) that increasingly take the burden of care off the shoulders of the hospital doctors who cannot cope with it.

Evidently, care of the dying and of the subsequently bereaved must be shared because of the demands that it imposes. This kind of team care is provided by the hospices, which have greatly increased in number over the past few years. Hospices provide an answer to the problem of institutionalised death. Care of the dying is a responsibility that hospitals do not want and it is often the hospice that takes it on. Here the dying patient and his family are cared for by a team of dedicated professionals: they are experts in pain control yet offer, in a family atmosphere, old-fashioned caring as opposed to frightening technology. The staff have the opportunity of exploring new approaches to the relief of pain, such as hypnotherapy and acupuncture, and they also have time to talk, areas which are not usually in the sphere of the hospital doctor. The social worker is one of the members of a team who attends the dying patient and his family, and after the death will visit them at home to help them through their grief and loneliness. Where possible the hospice offers home care, in the recognition that the environment in which he dies is of paramount importance to the dying: an indication of how their care of the dying extends beyond just care of the body, to care of the mind and spirit as well. They recognise the person as a whole human being, not just as a sick patient, and realise that to support the family is to support the dying man also; that by sharing their feelings with them they will help to allay their fears.

In times gone by most people died at home with their families around them, under whatever medical care was available. The body was laid out in the front room and left in the house for a while for relatives and friends to pay their last respects. All too often today the corpse is whisked away with unseemly haste, depriving the family of a precious span of mourning which later they often regret. There is nothing morbid in taking leave of the dead: the traditional wake is an important response not only to a real need to accept the reality of the death, but also a recognition that the time of death can be a very special one and one that should be shared.

There are good ways to die and bad ways to die; naturally we are not always in control of the manner of death, but where we are, we should handle it to its best advantage. If a man can die in an environment where he feels 'safe' and with someone he trusts beside him, it is an achievement that will help not only him but also his loved ones through their subsequent grief. It may be in his favourite chair, or his bedroom, or a chosen hospice; but his needs should be sensitively met wherever possible. If home care is possible, it is the ideal, and should be the goal of any improvement in health care.

Those who care for the dying bear witness to the fact that, when death is imminent, a dying person who has been sensitively cared for possesses an extraordinary peace, composure and clarity of mind, even though the time up to dying itself may have been hell. There is often an extraordinary calm that surrounds a dead person; when someone has looked ill and strained while they were dying, in death they can look beautifully peaceful, serene in a way that has to be seen to be believed: stress and worry lines disappear. By witnessing this phenomenon and sharing it, those who are present are possessed of a rare privilege. It will leave them with a more realistic view of their own eventual death as well as a wider understanding of human nature. The memory of it will help those who mourn.

Often people mellow as they are dying, and quite commonly seem to know the time of their death. In some cases the dying seem able even to control the time of their departure: it seems that they can keep themselves alive for the completion of a task, or for a reconciliation, then, with tranquil premonition, say their goodbyes and die. This underlines the fact that care of the dying is not a medical responsibility alone: it involves care of the spirit also. Hospices provide a good environment in which to die for those patients who are unable to be supported at home or where the illness requires full-time professional care. They can provide a worthy substitute for family closeness and offer spiritual and religious help that may be absent from home life.

Ideally hospices should be part of an entire hospital programme, which should also include team support units, increased domiciliary care, specially trained social workers and local council projects. The training of young doctors should cover the fields of dying and bereavement far more extensively than they do, and GPs should have the opportunity of attending seminars on the subject. Experimental training was carried out in Edinburgh, where 1000 students learned about the ethical, physical, spiritual and emotional problems in the care of the dying. They were, along with nurses, lectured to by hospice staff at the beginning of their medical training: at the end, six years later, they were asked to assess their reactions to this sensitisation in the light of a traditional training.

Many people who are in the grip of grief are confused by what is happening to them. Many of the physical symptoms of grief, and the anxiety caused by them, can be alleviated by explanation. Although grief takes different forms, many of the symptoms are common to the majority of mourners. Naturally it is not possible to follow the cut-and-dried course of treatment applicable, say, to infectious diseases; but, sadly, more often than not, instead of explaining the nature of the condition, the under-trained and over-worked GP prescribes tranquillizers and sleeping pills, which merely mask the basic problem. If people are told that their symptoms are normal, that the condition is called grief, that it may run this or that course, that they need to do this or that to help themselves, and that eventually the symptoms will pass or change, many of their fears will be eased.

Grief *is* a frightening process: many of its symptoms are disturbing and unexpected. They range through hallucinations, insomnia, death-wishes, weight loss, tension, stress, irrational fears, inability to concentrate, irritability, paranoia, exhaustion, restlessness, depression, anger, guilt, remorse, regret, confusion, etc. The range is formidable and people suffering from any of them need to be comforted and helped. In his book *Bereavement*, Colin Murray Parkes has written an illuminating account of the condition and process of grief (see page 191 for details).

The abandonment of much of the ritual of mourning has deprived the bereaved of a source of support and comfort. Many other cultures have well-defined rituals associated with death, based on accumulated wisdom about the needs of the bereft. The Victorians attached much importance to mourning: black was worn for a determined period of time, funerals were elaborate and the professionals involved – the undertakers and the clergy – took a pride in knowing their trade and in managing the matter sensitively and correctly, which indeed is frequently still the case. Often the family would lay the body out, and respects would be paid to the dead by mourning friends and relatives. This is far removed from our sketchy attempts at ritual and our unwillingness to be familiar with death and its ceremony. These things are not to be dismissed as morbid – they do satisfy a need of the bereft.

As society has changed, it has failed to realise that a change was needed in the handling of death and the after-care of the bereaved: it has chosen largely to turn a silent back on the problem. The 'mechanics' of death, the bureaucratic rigmarole involved in the registering of a death and the claim of the death grant, obtaining probate and so on, should be, if not common knowledge, then at least information which is easily available. This could be achieved by means of pamphlets, books and more open discussion; through education, and by information offered by the media. They could become far more familiar to the general public. (There is an excellent booklet available called *What to do when someone dies*, published by the Consumers Association.) People are sometimes unaware of how much help flowers and letters can be at the time of death: very often they take decisions to forestall them when they are feeling completely overwhelmed, distressed and confused. They may take decisions about burial or cremation in this stricken state which they afterwards regret bitterly. Flowers can bring the most extraordinarily powerful solace, and all the people interviewed for this book paid tribute to how healing and supportive were the letters of sympathy. If these things were more widely known there would be fewer regrets and problems over them: a re-established social pattern around death and bereavement would do much to help its victims.

The function of grief is not only to mourn loss: it has positive elements which show it to be a constructive process. It can lead through pain to a realisation that what is past is past, and help us to let go of it. It can lead forward through the natural process of suffering and searching, to the possibility of growth. Eventually it becomes essential, once the wounds have begun to heal, to rebuild. Memories, properly assimilated, play a great part in this rebuilding process. Many people who have been bereaved say that they are stronger, more sensitive, more complete people than they previously were. The consensus among the people interviewed for this book was that there were overwhelmingly positive things to come out of the experience of the death of somebody they loved. Over and over again, through a tale of real sadness, came this feeling of how lucky they were in other respects: almost a sense of privilege.

At the other extreme there is the danger of becoming over-indulgent in grief, and in turning into a 'professional mourner' as a protection from unwelcome changes and adjustments. There is a fine line between grief and self-pity. We can choose, if we like, to be – and remain – victims. But usually the gradual healing that comes with time, and a new set of expectations that can be incorporated with the memories of the dead person, can take people forward into what is for them often an unexpectedly rewarding new life. It helps people who grieve to feel that by living a positive and good life and by striving to be happy, that they are doing what would have pleased the person they loved, that the dead person would not want them to be miserable and tormented.

So many of the people in this book acknowledge gain through loss. They all expressed a desire – and indeed an increased ability – to help others in similar circumstances, whereas before they would not have known how to do so. It is possible that if we can see death and separation in terms of continuing life, we can experience the gain that *can* come through loss.

Through pain, acceptance can come: as pain recedes it leaves in its deep wake liberation from the past, and the possibility of leading a new life in the light of that experience. From pain to acceptance; from acceptance to growth; and a future which holds the possibility of deeper insight and understanding, of openness and personal freedom.

Many religious creeds acknowledge that, to face our own death with equanimity, we need to let go of anger, fear, guilt and shame. 'Perfect love casteth out fear' – the way to achieving a positive and complete vision of life and death. But whereas we will talk endlessly about love, we will not talk about death: we do not like being in the control of something so inevitable and unpredictable. The acknowledgement that death is an ever-present part of everyday life goes, at some deep level, some way to diminishing fear of the unknown. It also leads to the recognition that only by living through pain and suffering is it possible to grasp the paradox of grief as a strengthening process through which we can emerge as wiser and more complete people.

The stories that the people tell in this book are profoundly moving: they will touch those who read them into an understanding of their feelings. I hope that they will offer not only enlightenment to those who have not been bereaved, but consolation and comfort to those who have been.

Then there is the astonishing movement called creation. It can only be in total negation; it cannot be in the passage of time, nor can space cover it. There must be complete death, total destruction, for it to be.

Krishnamurti's Notebook

1

SANDRA:
her stillborn daughter

Sandra and Eric live on the outskirts of a large county town. She is thirty-three and a temporary supply teacher; he is thirty-five and works as an executive for the GPO. Three years ago, after many conception difficulties, she became pregnant and, although there were problems with the pregnancy, she came to full term. She was admitted to hospital in labour, but the baby, a little girl, died before delivery. A few months later she had an early miscarriage, but she is now the proud mother of Pamela, who is five months old.

Death borders upon our birth, and our cradle
Stands in the grave.

Joseph Hall (1574–1656), *Epistles*

I'd had difficulty conceiving and it had taken me eight years to get that far on in pregnancy. My doctor's advice immediately after delivery of the stillborn child was not to use any contraception: he said, 'The best cure for you is another baby.' I don't know whether that was right, or whether I needed more time.

I was very calm at first: the calm, at the actual time during the delivery and immediately afterwards upset me. I was banking on them letting me go home the next morning and they wouldn't let me go home for days because I hadn't cried yet. There was a midwife there but they never contacted her, otherwise she would have come and given me a follow-up at home. So the only plan I made when I was having my second baby, Pamela, was that I was coming home as soon as I had had the baby.

When I started labour I knew it wasn't right; I couldn't feel the baby moving. When I went into hospital nobody actually said to me that there was no hope, that the baby was dead: the doctor thought he could hear a heartbeat. I remember thinking, 'You're actually going to have this baby'; I didn't believe it myself then. It upsets me now that they can't tell you what's happening. My husband asked, and they told him that the baby was in a distressed condition and they couldn't hear the heartbeat. But nobody ever told me that. They could have done a caesarian then; there might have been a chance, but they didn't. I've a lot of bones to pick with the hospital, but there's nothing you can do.

They don't give a stillborn child a name, and they certainly didn't advise me to. It would always have been Sarah Ann because the first specialist who gave us any hope at all of conceiving liked those names and we told him we'd call her that. I saw her: she was all wrapped up in green sterile towels. I didn't hold her, but I do wish I had. She was so beautiful. If she'd only just lived for a few minutes. I need to talk and talk about it: you've got to talk it out. At first you don't take it in, you're numb. And they leave you on your own. You're so alone in there: they keep away from you and you feel like a leper. What you want is people to talk with, to cry with, to be next to you.

Your husband comes in and he wants to cry. He doesn't want your tears, he wants his own tears. You feel such a failure: you've failed to produce the goods. You can't give comfort because you want comfort yourself so much. The only people who really understand are the ones who have actually been through it. I did talk to the doctor but apparently he thought I was being neurotic. He answered a lot of my questions – but perhaps there should have been a social worker or a health visitor there to do that.

What I found in that hospital was a complete lack of communication between members of staff: I had a pair of twins brought along to me and asked if they were mine. The physiotherapist came in and asked where my baby was, was she in special care? how old was she? – she didn't know what had happened. They let a girl from the ante-natal classes I'd been to come in to see me without telling her what had happened.

My husband wouldn't see Sarah and he's always regretted it. I think after an experience like that one's next or surviving child is doubly precious: one is so aware of the thin line between life and death. Most people when they have babies think, 'Oh yes, it's come along, it's normal,' and they drag it up – they haven't a clue how lucky they are. The doctor asked if they could do a post mortem and we said yes: I wanted to know, I had to know what had happened. She was a perfect baby girl: there was nothing wrong. I wanted to see her before she was buried, but I just couldn't: I didn't know what to expect. I didn't know how tidy they'd make her afterwards. But as soon as she was buried I felt a lot easier.

We had a little service at the cemetery, standing around the grave. Our first instinct was to have her cremated, and I went down to the undertaker to register the death. Apparently for cremation they have to have two signatures on the death certificate which nobody at the hospital had mentioned. Once you've got a death certificate you can't get another one without a lot of performance, so we couldn't have her cremated. I spent that whole week in turmoil because nobody seemed to be able to tell me what should happen. One person said they put them in a grave with somebody else, someone else said they just have a big communal grave. I've often felt since that if they'd just given us a pamphlet at the hospital and explained it all, it would have been so much easier for us. You don't have to be told by someone; if you read it it's clear cut and clinical. You don't know what to ask, things don't occur to you because you're in such a state.

We both wanted to be there when she was buried and they said at the undertaker's, 'Oh, nobody goes, nobody bothers.' We said, 'We don't care about anybody else, we want to be there.' He said, 'All right, it's at nine o'clock in the morning,' and we said, 'All right, we'll be there; just tell us which morning.' So in the end he took us at half past three on a

Monday afternoon. It was a glorious day – it was so hot that Eric was in his shirt sleeves with no tie on, and I felt it was rather disrespectful, particularly with the undertakers in their black. We had nine red roses, one for each month, and my sister brought some silly lace shoes so we tied those on and put them in with her. I felt the temptation then to have a look, but I didn't. I feel she's there now, and as soon as she was buried I could relax.

That was the following week: in between I just couldn't stop. I was picking raspberries endlessly, I was restless all the time; if I lay down I just cried. One thing I learned then and still do, is to cry quietly. It's not such a relief but one needs to cry. My husband was a support in some ways, and not in others: his need for comfort is physical, and I was useless then. I felt such a failure: I hadn't produced a baby and I couldn't be a good wife. I just wasn't anything. It's difficult to explain. We find it too painful to talk about with each other. I felt he didn't really understand, because I'd spent most of the pregnancy doing nothing because it hadn't been a terribly easy one in some ways. But at the end everything got to a peak of getting ready for the baby and I felt then that everything was going to be all right. We were planning ahead, we'd booked a holiday with the baby in mind, everything was geared up to having the baby and suddenly there was this great empty gap.

I didn't know whether to go back to work and teach – I didn't know that I could cope with other people's children. I don't think people appreciate the great effort you have to make to go into a babywear shop and buy something for someone else's baby. They don't realise what it does to you, to actually hold someone else's baby and coo at him. Fortunately, I did meet one good friend who had a little girl about the same time and said, 'If you ever feel you want to hold her, come on over.' I remember once I went to a play group and that was a real effort – and there was a baby there just like Sarah, with a little curly head just like hers. I could have picked her up and stolen her. I had to drive over to my friend and give her little girl a quick cuddle. I can appreciate that some people don't want to ever hold another baby, at

4

least for a long time, but I felt I did want to hold a baby, a little girl. Everybody I knew had little boys!

Everyone is so wary with you for the first few weeks, and then suddenly it's gone from their minds. Two months afterwards someone said wasn't it about time I was pregnant again: only two months. It's one of the loneliest of losses, because you are the only person who has had a relationship with the baby. You've got no real memory of the child, the person. I can never feel really sad for anyone who dies who has had a life: my father-in-law has just died but he was seventy-six, he had his chances of happiness; Sarah never had her chance. If only she had. I feel sad in a way for Pamela now because I can never give her a big sister again. I'll do my best to give her a little sister or brother but she can never have a big sister. It's irreplaceable. Yet so many people think that now I've got Pamela everything's all right. Even my doctor at the hospital said that I should forget the other child. But she's real to me: she's my daughter and she's Pamela's older sister. I shall tell Pamela about her.

Every month I find that I wind up, and when I look at the calendar it's always around the date in the month that she died. We usually go up to the cemetery then and take flowers from the garden and then I wind down again. We're only there a few minutes; a lot of people think it's morbid to go up there and that I shouldn't go. Very few of the little graves are tended and I just don't understand that. I understand if you're far away but I like her to know she's still cared about.

When I see little girls of around the same age as Sarah it does bring it home to me. There are times when we do feel, particularly now with Pamela, that there is an emptiness there. There should be four of us – when we go to the seaside, Sarah should have been there as well. Poor Pamela – occasionally I have called her Sarah. They say she was very like Sarah when she was born. I can sometimes see it when she's asleep, the eyes and the mouth are so like her. I always think Sarah was prettier, she had curls and eyelashes when she was born, beautiful long eyelashes down her cheeks.

I hope it won't complicate my relationship with Pamela: I think I will always have a much deeper relationship with her.

I know that she will probably disappoint us when she grows up but I don't think I could ever stop loving her. I suppose that's idealising Sarah: she will always be the perfect baby. When we hear babies screaming in the supermarket we look at each other and say, 'Sarah would never have done that.' Funnily enough Pamela never does it either – she's such a perfect baby in so many ways.

I haven't really found anyone I can talk to, then or subsequently. Not someone who could be there when I needed them. My mother lives far away: that's why you're getting it all now. I still cry at night sometimes, even after having Pamela. I really shouldn't think of what might have been, but it's difficult not to. It's an irreplaceable loss. When I had Pamela I made a point of not crying when the doctor who delivered Sarah came to see me because I was known as the girl who cried every time I saw him. I had a caesarian with her – I was terrified of a natural birth. Sarah's delivery was a forceps, that on top of everything; it was terrible knowing it was all for nothing, just a futile exercise. I feel really sorry for girls who know their babies are dead for days before and still have to go through it. There was a girl in there who'd known her baby was dead for a week, and she didn't cry afterwards. She said she'd done all her crying beforehand; I couldn't understand how she felt.

I felt so guilty. I felt it was all my fault, I thought I'd failed her. It was obvious, as she was a perfect baby – nothing wrong with her, that it must have been me. I still feel that the fault was mine.

I took sleeping pills for quite a long time afterwards. I think I drank more. Otherwise I didn't take drugs – I was determined I would try and get pregnant again. Which I did, only to miscarry at fourteen weeks. I felt far worse after the miscarriage, physically and mentally, than I did after the stillbirth: the birth had left me with the hope that I would become pregnant again quickly, and that they would know from last time what to look out for: I'd still got hope. The miscarriage seemed to destroy that hope. In a funny way I'd refused to admit that I was pregnant. I told myself that it wasn't a baby I was having. It was the same with Pamela, we prepared nothing for her, everything was left up in the loft. I hoped everything would go all right but I couldn't commit myself to thinking 'the baby': I felt I'd been conned the last time, and I always suspected that something would go wrong.

I felt particularly angry with God after the miscarriage: I felt depressed the following morning in hospital and the tears were rolling. Sister was doing her rounds and she said, 'What's the matter with you?' and I told her and she said, 'Oh, never mind, you've got another one at home. You've been pregnant before.' I said, 'I've been pregnant before but she was still-born.' 'Oh, what went wrong there?' 'Nothing.' 'There must have been something wrong with the baby.' 'Well they tell me she was a perfect baby, that there was nothing wrong with her at all.' 'Oh there must have been something wrong, it's God's way of getting rid of the mistakes in the world; it's nothing to worry about.' I looked at her coldly and nearly told her what to do in four letter words. All the time she was talking there was a mongol girl in the ward yelling her head off and I thought, 'If that's God's idea of perfection it's time he went back to school.' I've never been particularly religious but I would very much like to be: I would love to find some inner peace. But it's all just not consistent.

I would like to feel that Sarah was somewhere else. The children of a friend of mine didn't really understand why I hadn't got my baby, and when their granny died suddenly a month afterwards one of them said, 'Oh, Nana's gone to look after Sandra's baby.' I like to think that she is looking after Sarah somewhere. Children hit the nail on the head: out of the mouths of babes and infants ... One of them asked if I would take her to Sarah's grave one day; I could see her mother biting her finger nails, but I said 'Yes, if you'd like to go, we'll take some flowers', which coming from me is something because it took a great effort even to take my parents up there. That bit up there is my daughter and it's all I've got of her and I don't want to share her with anyone even if it is my mother and father. It's the only tangible thing left.

She's got her own grave – they have some tiny little plots where the rent has run out. Every month that we go up there there seem to be six or seven more. So an awful lot of people go through it, because it's from twenty-eight weeks to the first week of life, unless they've been christened and they get a proper burial. I find it very difficult to accept that in the eyes of the church they are not people, they are in limbo. I don't believe in that.

I started back at work, supply teaching, but had to rest when I became pregnant again, and then I miscarried. I felt suicidal at times afterwards. One morning I just didn't want to wake up, so I took a couple of sleeping pills and just slept. My husband rang up and I couldn't be bothered to answer the phone so he came home in a flat spin. He was terribly upset. But that was what I wanted – sleep, oblivion, and preferably a drugged sleep because I wouldn't manage it on my own. They say sleep is a great healer, time being the other one; so they say. I don't want it to heal, quite honestly, because if it heals I shall forget. Perhaps it's a sign that I'm not completely over it, but I don't want to forget; she was my daughter.

I always used to have flowers in the house and it's only this year I've started cutting flowers for indoors again. Before Sarah they were always secondary, but now they are so important to me. And I notice I've started to laugh just for the sake of laughing. You can't not laugh when there's a baby around. It helps to keep smiling. Her routine still has to be there, she has to be fed, and that's what keeps me going.

When we came home after the stillbirth I had nothing: an empty house. All the things were in the bedroom, her pram and everything, and I closed the door. Eric opened it: he didn't want to shut her out of our lives completely, just like that. I went straight into the room and picked up the things she would have worn and we both cried. It really took an effort later to put Pamela in some of the things Sarah would have worn.

It did put a strain on our marriage. I remember Eric told me after a few months to snap out of it. I was just about ready to walk out then, because I did think he was expecting a bit much. That was when I learnt to cry quietly: it used to disturb him if I sobbed, so I still cry quietly. When I was pregnant with Pamela I used to go through the nightmares again, the actual delivery and so on. I just used to lie and cry. He never noticed. Those strains have been replaced by the strains of having a young baby around and not being as young as I probably ought to be. I find that I'm very tired, and also he's going through pressures at work.

I've still got all the letters we had after Sarah died. That's something I did learn: we appreciated the fact that people took the trouble just to put pen to paper, and since then whenever anyone has died I've always done so. It's a difficult thing to do but just to say 'I'm sorry, and my thoughts are with you' helps so much. I find it a lot easier to share other people's grief now. It's true that it gives one understanding.

I just wish we had more memories. We have a few, a very, very few. There was one time when Eric put his ear to my tummy to hear her heartbeat and got kicked! Just a few things like that, but most of it is nightmares. I wonder what I'm letting Pamela in for – it's a hard world and some people seem to get all the bruises. There are some bruises that leave scars.

In a lot of ways I don't think I was helped through it – I got through it on my own. There were a few people who rang up and Eric said it was an expensive phone bill for two people just to cry on the phone – not that he minded, but he has got a cynical side. Some people surprised me by how they felt for me and I have felt closer to them, my elder brother for one, who was terribly upset. But he's had his problems and his understanding comes through his own suffering; he knows how it feels.

I need to talk about it far more than I've been allowed to. But it's only people who know how it feels that you can communicate with. I feel I could cope if anything happened to Eric now, because I've got Pamela. It gives me a much better hold on life. If I'd lost her I would have had nothing. If Pamela had gone wrong I knew exactly what I was going to do: drive the car off the docks. It was about the only plan I made, that and coming out of hospital as soon as I could get on my feet. And they said about Pamela, 'Oh, she's such a happy baby, it comes from having a happy contented mother.' If only they'd known what was going on in my mind most of the time.

I would very much have liked a photo of Sarah but I felt it was too morbid to ask. We'd got the camera there because Eric had been hoping that everything would be all right. But I've a couple of photos, adverts of baby things that I'd cut out and I've got in a recipe book that no-one else is likely to open, which I do periodically look at. I found I got most consolation out of the babygro that she would have worn out of hospital. After she was buried, that afternoon we put everything up in the loft, but I found that I would go up and get that out and just hold it for a few minutes. It was a kind of comfort – like a child with its rag.

All the time you want to know that you're normal: when does the crying stop? If you know it's permissible to cry that long you don't feel so bad. But you get the feeling you're so abnormal; there's nobody to tell you 'Well, of course it's normal and you'll have these feelings and you need to go through all this to get over it.' There's nobody to guide you.

OK, it's God's way, but what about all those people that seem to go through life with no suffering, no crisis: for the majority of people the biggest crisis is when the bread man doesn't turn up. We're at an age now when a lot of friends are into their second marriages and I think, 'What's wrong with us that we stay together?' The answer is that the suffering we have had has bonded us – everything else seems so trivial in comparison.

I would have been helped so much by reading something about stillbirth and how to manage it. There were one or two articles I found, and I started writing down how I felt about it. Going through it again step by step all the bitterness came out. That was about five months afterwards, after the miscarriage. But I should have been able to find out about cremation and burial – I expect it varies regionally: however, I'm glad we had her buried, I think it's more positive.

There were so many things to remind me of Sarah that year – there was a television programme, with a girl who had had a stillbirth; and then all the other things that happened to me, like the miscarriage: life really chucks it at you sometimes.

2

JUDITH:
her new-born son

Judith is thirty-five and she married Alex when she was thirty. They live in London and nearly three years ago she had her first baby, Laura, who is now a robust toddler. Two years later she became pregnant again and ten months ago went into premature labour: she was delivered of a little boy, David, but he died after an hour and a half. Six months later she had a miscarriage at twelve weeks. Even though she is a strong and positive person she still cannot talk about David without weeping. Judith is a layout artist by training and has since gone back to work part-time, which has helped to keep up her morale while she plucks up her courage to make a decision as to whether to try to have another baby.

There is a reaper whose name is Death
And, with his sickle keen,
He reaps the bearded grain at a breath,
And the flowers that grow between.

Longfellow: *The Reaper and the Flowers*

Although it happened ten months ago now, in some ways it feels like miles and miles away. Talking about it brings it up again: I'm a cry-baby and that's one of the things that has always helped me.

It all started in the middle of the night. I thought I'd got indigestion – I couldn't believe that I was in labour, the sharp pains didn't feel like it. I was seven months pregnant to the day. We rang the hospital and had to get an ambulance –

Alex couldn't come with me because Laura was asleep upstairs, so I couldn't have him with me. I've got relatives who are great buddies who live only a few streets away, but I couldn't ring them at three in the morning; you simply can't. However, Alex managed to get to the hospital for the birth.

I was rushed off and the baby arrived at six in the morning. It was terribly fast and there was nothing they could do to stop it. All the staff were specially trained to cope with that sort of disaster and they were so sympathetic. They told me how it did happen sometimes, and how I must cry as much as possible and not bottle it up. They kept saying, 'Cry, cry for God's sake keep crying; don't worry about us, you mustn't bottle it up.' They were so nice to me, and their kindness started something very constructive for me: it was because they were so nice that they gave me a direction. I know from what I've read that in some hospitals it's completely the reverse: their attitude is, 'Pull yourself together.' Unfortunately they are light years behind.

He died about an hour and a half after he was born. There was nothing physically wrong with him, no brain damage or anything. It was just that, at thirty weeks, he had immature lungs and they couldn't get him to breathe. I could hear them trying to resuscitate him and then they whizzed out saying, 'We must ventilate him and get him on an incubator.' They never told me, but I suspect they never even put him on the ventilator, because you can't make a baby of that age breathe after such a long time without it getting brain damage.

I didn't see him afterwards: I chose not to because I saw him when he was born and he looked so lovely. My mother-in-law took a photo of him when he was dead and she wanted me to see it afterwards, but I still can't see it. I don't regret not seeing him afterwards: she thought the photograph would help, but I've got my memory and that was all I needed, because he was so perfect and he looked lovely. He was lying on my stomach as they were cutting the cord and that's just how I like to remember him. The nursing officer in charge tried very hard to get me to see him after he died and said, 'You may very well regret it; are you sure you don't want to see him?' The nurses pushed quite hard too. I explained that I had seen him and that was the memory I wanted. Because I'd had a chance to see him like that he was absolutely real to me, and I didn't want to see the sadness of it all.

We called him David and we had a proper funeral for him, a very small one. I couldn't face the funeral for a couple of weeks so I went down to my mother's and stayed with her. When I came back I was absolutely determined to get back to being as normal as possible, because the longer I put it off the more difficult it would become – it's far more difficult to face people: it embarrasses them as well as embarrassing you. I had to do it: I was acutely aware that I had to try to be as normal as possible and be able to talk to them about it, because otherwise they wouldn't know what to say. They didn't. I had to make the first move always.

They didn't want to talk about the baby with me, I found. I wanted to talk about him all the time. I needed to, I had to get it out of my system. I had been pregnant all that time, and it was real to me; he had been kicking inside me and suddenly there wasn't a baby, and nothing to show for it except a little white box. Dreadful. And my hormones were still going – that was the most painful thing. The craving for my baby was intense, I was even awash with milk. There was milk absolutely everywhere for two solid weeks. I was very lucky with the midwife then, she was marvellous and constituted another link in the chain of help. She had had one miscarriage and one premature birth at five months and she had been through the same thing with the milk: all that milk, and nothing to feed with it; it's ironic.

When I got pregnant again, I lost the baby at twelve weeks, suddenly; they couldn't stop it. I've always been twitchy about having a miscarriage, it's always been the one thing I've been scared of. I almost feel I brought it on myself this time. Obviously I was scared after losing David so far on: you think, 'My God, I've got to go through that again.' Of course I've been assured that you can't bring anything like that on yourself, but I got myself into a state thinking I was going to lose it. It was almost as if it was psychological; it's amazing what the mind can do to the body. And since the miscarriage my hormones have been upside down.

It's odd, but afterwards I never needed sleeping pills or tranquillizers. I slept like a log. I did have rotten dreams that went on for several weeks – a lot of them were just unpleasant dreams about nothing in particular. But the week after the miscarriage I did dream for several nights running about losing the baby, and about babies covered in blood. They've gone now, though. It's not just the emotional thing of losing a baby, and then having another pregnancy, it's that my hormones are so mixed up. I always dream dreadfully in pregnancy, it's one of the first things that indicates that I'm pregnant – I have awful nightmares, and I wake up exhausted. Subsequently, though, because I managed to let it out, to cry, to talk to people, I exhausted myself, so that at night I did sleep, and except for those dreams I was able to actually rest.

My husband was a fantastic help to me: he's very involved in the whole thing and he's a very understanding person. He comes from a large family and they have all been brought up to be very sympathetic, and to help – they're not remotely male chauvinist pigs! They've been taught to share in the home, and he is far more help to me than most men would have been. Of course, it's a dreadful loss for him, too. I often think I have taken much more of it on myself and have forgotten about his feelings. He has supported me so much and put up with my ups and downs. The worst thing is that I get to screaming pitch with poor Laura: a two-year-old is very demanding and you can't switch off for a moment. She doesn't understand what happened and there's no point in trying to explain. She's heard me talking to people about it but she's never really taken it in. It was so sad, because we had only just started to tell her about the baby – we thought two or three months' build-up was enough. She adores babies and she is still mad on them. She came to visit me in the hospital and she was sitting on my bed saying happily, 'Mummy and Daddy are having a baby soon.' I felt so upset for her because I wanted to have two children together and it brought it home to me in one bitter lesson that you cannot arrange your life as you exactly want it. You can't really plan.

Laura didn't come to the funeral, she wouldn't have known

what it was about. I think she would have been very confused with me crying, my mother-in-law crying and my sister-in-law crying. My poor mother couldn't face coming to the funeral: she is a worse cry-baby than I am. Funerals upset her a lot anyway – she's had her fair share in her time – but she felt she would upset me, more than anything. She wouldn't be able to be a tower of strength, she would be crying too much for me.

When I came back from the hospital the house was awash with flowers. So many people had sent me flowers and that was lovely: it was a concrete acknowledgement that something had happened. People were very generous, and I love flowers anyway. They helped me a lot. The thing that helped me most though was trying to get back to being as normal as possible and doing everyday things like shopping and running the house. And talking to friends: although one of the greatest sadnesses of my life is that two of my oldest friends have never acknowledged it happening.

When I lost the baby, I thought, 'Oh my God, this is going to be awful for everybody; they're going to be ringing up and saying, "When's the baby coming?" or "Has it arrived yet?"' I wanted to forestall that, not only from my point of view in having to explain, but also to spare them the embarrassment. So I sat down in hospital and wrote letters to all my friends telling them what had happened. I had letters back from everyone, masses of letters too from people I didn't even know very well, really sweet letters that made me howl buckets. But what a help they were: I felt loved and liked and I knew people were feeling for me. People I hardly knew would stop me in the supermarket and say, 'How sorry I am,' and I thought that was fantastic. But I never had letters from either of these two old friends, I never had a phone call. Months later one of them rang me up and twittered on and chatted but didn't want to ask anything or really want to know how I was. She wouldn't talk about the baby at all and rang off terribly quickly, and I felt rather like saying, 'Stuff you.' The following February she rang again and said, 'How are you?' and I said, 'Actually I'm pregnant again.' The relief in her voice! She said, 'I hope you have a little boy this time,' and I said, 'I had a little boy last time.' She immediately changed the subject. I didn't hear from her again and she doesn't know I had a miscarriage. I just don't want to ring her. She's been through difficult times herself and been close to death with a heart operation, but she doesn't want to admit that it's happened.

My other friend has a little boy who's a year older than Laura and had her second child just before I lost David. She never acknowledged it at all. I suppose death has not hit her, even though she lost both her parents. I feel I never want to get in touch with either of them again: perhaps that's a petty way to think, but they're not giving me any support at all, and I'm not hanging around saying, 'I want to be supported.' It wasn't as if they were just acquaintances, they were long-standing friends. I just couldn't believe it, I still can't to this day. That unhappy phrase comes to mind: you know who your friends are at a time of crisis. You certainly see how the sheep divide from the goats.

Only a matter of hours after David died my husband said to me, 'We must think about the funeral.' My immediate reaction was to reject it totally, but a few hours later I agreed with the idea. Because then it's more real to you, it's proof to you and to the world that it's happened. I'm terribly glad that I did it, now; I would feel awful if I hadn't done it. It wasn't that I was rejecting the idea that I'd got a funeral as such, it was that I was rejecting the idea that I'd got a funeral at all. It was too unreal at that actual moment. Looking back, it would have been dreadful to have left his body in the hospital, which is what some people do. It was such a shock at the time that I couldn't accept that it had happened. One often reads that people have premature babies that die, but it doesn't happen to you, does it? Except that it does. I didn't want to think of the funeral because I didn't want to accept what had happened. But it was by far the best thing to have it: I dreaded it, but after it was over I felt so much better: it was a lovely afternoon, it was bright and sunny and we came back and all had tea in the garden and were able to talk and laugh together.

We had a service at the crematorium and there was

something that happened that I found very upsetting, although I can laugh about it now. Whether the vicar hadn't been told what kind of funeral it was, or what, we don't know. We didn't have a funeral car; we had it as simple as possible and we took the box in the back of our car and walked in with it ourselves. We must have looked so pathetic with this little white box. It didn't look like a coffin and it just broke my heart to see it sitting there on the stand. This vicar was so embarrassed – a vicar, who should be involved with death, and he didn't know what to say. He obviously hadn't prepared anything and he huffed and fluffed for a few minutes and then half-realised what was going on. He didn't know what to say and proceeded to give the most appalling talk. His theme was that it was quite a good thing that it had happened because through it I would find God. Now I'm not strongly religious but this finally disillusioned me. He made up some silly parables about people finding God through suffering and thanking God for it: I thought, 'Oh, yes, well if that is how God acts I don't want to know.' It may be very blasphemous but I'd rather have my baby than find God I'm afraid.

About three weeks after I lost David, by sheer chance the local vicar popped in and had a cup of tea. My sister-in-law rang and I mentioned something about the baby and he heard it of course. He said, 'What happened?' and I told him that I had lost the baby. The poor man was so embarrassed: again, a vicar, and I thought that vicars were meant to be able to comfort the bereaved. They're supposed to be good at it, but he didn't know what to say and couldn't give me any of the words of comfort which should come rolling off the tongue. It was his job, and he failed at it. It makes me pretty anti-church I'm afraid.

A little later I went to a self-help discussion on stillbirth. A girl there had had a stillbirth a few years ago and we talked out our experiences. We all felt that not enough is talked about these things, and that if it happens to someone else you can help them by talking with them. I found it rather distressing, though; it was too soon afterwards: I felt quite brave as I walked in, but it set me off again. However, it was quite constructive and they were very sympathetic. It wasn't a bad experience, because they were on my side: they just wanted to understand. The girl who had had the stillbirth said, 'People say that if you've been through something like that, you're meant to be a better person afterwards, but I don't think I am.' In fact she said she was horrible to her husband and almost broke up her marriage because she took it out on him. She had a child who was the same age as Laura and what scared the life out of me was that a year later she became very disturbed and had to see a child psychologist. They decided that the child had been very distressed by the reactions of her parents to the loss of the baby. The marriage survived but she had taken it to the brink by working out her anger on her husband: the last person you want to be angry with, but I'm afraid you always do take it out on your nearest and dearest simply because they are your nearest.

It's ten months now and I suppose things are beginning to heal. Yet something very small can bring it all back. Having miscarried on top of it all is not exactly helpful. I feel very muddled: at one moment I feel that I must have another baby because I want Laura to have a sibling and the next moment I don't know if I could face it again. Obviously I'm frightened of the whole thing happening again, although the doctors say there's no reason why it should. But it can happen, and with the miscarriage on top of David's death, it's rather like the lightning striking twice.

After David's death I went to specialists because I had had migraines in my pregnancies: I was searching and searching to try and pin it on the idea that they had triggered off the premature labour. I was desperately trying to find a reason. I needed a reason. It seemed such a waste of time, and I felt so angry. I had done so much work and I had this relationship with my baby, and there was nothing to show for it. My anger was partly against fate for treating me like that, although I wasn't really indulging in self-pity. Everyone wallows in self-pity now and again but that wasn't really it. It was just such a waste of time and energy and effort and creativity. I was cross with myself too because I wasn't in charge of my destiny, so to speak. I was going to have my two little children nice and neatly, two years between them, and I wasn't able to organise myself. I'm rather an organised sort of person and I was angry with myself for not being organised. My sister-in-law had just had her second child and he would have been four months older than David: Laura gets on like a house on fire with her first child and it was all a bit too perfect. Much too dangerous, imagining you can play with fate. So it was anger with myself as well as with circumstances for dealing me such a blow.

I felt more guilt with the miscarriage in a way; I almost feel I brought it on myself because I was so afraid of it happening, which is totally unconstructive and stupid: not guilt that I had done anything to cause it. There wasn't anything to pin it on and I needed a reason desperately, I still need a reason and I'm not going to get one. I feel that nobody's trying to find out why neo-natal deaths occur: they are quite common and they can't explain them. It's amazing that they don't even know what triggers off the birth – it's such an elementary thing: we can get to the moon, we live in the technological world of bionic man and it seems incredible that they can't tell why a birth is premature.

Luckily I hadn't got David's room ready, and I had got all the baby clothes anyway, of Laura's, so it wasn't like a first baby, going out and buying the nappy buckets and the cot and so on. At least I've got Laura: and if I never have another one I'll have her. It's a major comfort. Although she's taxing my energy, I'd have gone out of my mind if I hadn't had her, because she at least kept me going: you have to keep going with a two-year-old, they've got to be fed and watered and occupied and loved and that keeps you on the straight and narrow. I was surprised when David was born at the enormous wave of love that I felt, because babies as such don't make me feel broody. I shouldn't have been surprised because it's natural, this immense maternal feeling of love. I felt so sorry for him, because I knew he wasn't going to make it, I just knew he couldn't. I almost didn't want him to survive, in a way, because I was so scared that he would be brain damaged. Often it comes out in later life; they told me that at the hospital, they underlined it, I suppose to make me feel better. I don't know how I'd cope with a handicapped child. I suppose it has changed me in some ways: maybe I can put up with more. Probably I can understand more and sympathise with other people's problems, knowing what they're going through and being able to help.

We didn't have a plaque put up at the cemetery: I didn't think of it at the time. It wouldn't mean anything to me to go there because I have my own memories of him. The birth was a very good one: I was totally aware of what was going on, and I really quite enjoyed it. I felt I was constructive about it all: I saw him and that's what I remember. Sometimes I look at a friend of mine who had her second child the month that David was due – we were going neck and neck – and I look at her baby and think, 'Oh, God, David would be at that stage now'. But it's not constructive to think like that.

I don't know how I'll feel on his anniversary: I've often thought about it because it is coming nearer. I wonder what my reaction will be: I think I will be upset – we're a very anniversary-minded family. My family support all in all has been marvellous: there's a feeling of being loved, and that counts for more than anything. I talk to my mother on the phone a lot, and my mother-in-law who I see quite often has been absolutely super to me. She cried with me, she felt angry about it with me. To her, the fact of losing the life of a baby was very upsetting. My own mother felt more upset for *me* for being so upset. My mother-in-law was also very upset at the loss of a grandson: to her he was the one grandson who died. She has drawn up a family tree and added his name to it. To her, it's terribly real. That's why she took the photograph.

He was a real person even though he was so tiny. At his birth he was a total, complete person. That's why it's so awful not to have him, not to have anything to show for it afterwards. You've seen the potential and the future and you've lost it. You've been bearing the baby throughout all that time, and it's so sad.

3

JACKY:
her son, a cot death

Jacky and Stephen have been married for fourteen years and now live, after a series of moves, in a small county town. Stephen, thirty-five, is a salesman and Jacky, who is a year younger, looks after their two daughters, Lucy who is nine and Sophie who is five and a half. Seven years ago, when Lucy was two, Jacky had a little boy called Thomas who died in his sleep when he was seven weeks old – it was a cot death. Four months later she had a miscarriage, but subsequently had her second daughter. Neither of the two girls knew of the existence of their brother at the time of the interview.

The wind bloweth where it listeth, and thou hearest the sound thereof, but canst not tell whence it cometh, and whither it goeth: so is everyone that is born of the Spirit.

The Gospel according to St John, 3, viii

There was almost exactly two years between Lucy and Thomas, which I felt was lovely and very according to plan. I think people don't understand about cot deaths unless they have had any involvement in one: basically you have usually got a very healthy baby – it seems to happen to babies who are above average weight, and it is usually boys. Thomas was quite chubby and showed promise of being quite a hefty baby. I had absolutely no idea, no inkling even. It was something I'd never heard of, I didn't know it happened, a cot death. I had no idea what it was called or anything.

We had a ghastly week that week, really awful, because on the previous Sunday – he died on the Friday – Lucy, who was just two, swallowed a bottle of aspirins. There was a horrible panic; we had to rush her into hospital and have her pumped out. They were a little worried about her so they kept her in until the Tuesday. During this time Thomas took very much a back seat: friends looked after him for me, then Lucy came home, still not really well. At the end of that week my sister was getting married and Lucy was a bridesmaid so I had lots of rushing around to do for that too. As the week progressed a friend offered to have Thomas for me on the Saturday because he was rather tiny to take to a wedding in London. I was a bit flustered because Lucy was still being sick, so I rang the midwife. Thomas was sitting in the corner of the settee, screaming his head off. He was a bit of a screamer un- fortunately, although I hate to say it; but he wasn't par- ticularly easy, and I had two to cope with anyway. I went up to get Lucy from her rest and said to Thomas, 'It won't do you any harm to have a yell for five minutes.' I told the midwife that he had a bit of a runny nose, and apparently, it now transpires, that often is the case before a cot death. She gave him a little inspection and said, 'There's nothing wrong with you. I'll bring some nose drops down because that's the best thing I can offer you. There's nothing really, he's fine.' So that dismissed him as being A1 and consequently we concen- trated on Lucy. So I had absolutely no reason to suspect anything, even more so because somebody who had got medical experience had looked at him that day.

That night I got him down at about ten thirty to feed him and all was quite well. As we had got friends there he stayed up rather longer than he should have done, but he was bouncing on my knee and was perfectly happy. We went to bed about midnight and my husband found him in the morning. All I can really remember about that particular week is being absolutely shattered. I remember going to bed every night feeling as though I hadn't got any energy at all. Thomas used to sleep in his basket and Stephen, my husband, used to take the basket downstairs in the morning, prepare his food and bring him back up with his bottle, the idea being that he wouldn't initially wake me up by yelling.

This particular morning he had apparently picked up the basket and carried it downstairs; he went and heated the bottle up and just happened to glance at him, and he was blue. He tried to give him the kiss of life, but it didn't work, so he rang our GP. This was about five-thirty, and he came immediately. He was absolutely super: in fact the same thing had happened to him the previous year; he had lost his little girl in the same way. He confirmed there was nothing he could do, and then they came and woke me up: there was my husband and my GP and in that blurred state that you're in when you first wake up, you can't quite put everything together. I couldn't make out what was happening, I didn't understand what was going on. Stephen said, 'It's Thomas, he's dead' and it just didn't register, I have no idea what I thought, it was unreal. It was just a sort of horrible nightmare. I can see myself flying down the stairs and I can't explain it. It was awful. He looked all blue and cold. I cuddled him and he was so cold. All I can remember is that his mouth was open, his eyelashes were stuck together and his eyes were a bit sticky. I said to my GP, 'Why has this happened? I don't understand.' As he had had a cold I'd propped his basket up in order that any mucus wouldn't get back into his throat, which was a precaution as far as I was concerned. He said, 'I can't explain it to you' and by this time he was in tears because it was a repeat performance of what had happened to him a year before. It's a horrible, horrible blow. It's such a nasty experience it's difficult to describe it.

My husband was magnificent. I don't know how I would have coped without him. We don't talk about it now, it's seven years ago now, but I don't think that he doesn't care because he does, he cares deeply and I think that is why he doesn't talk about it. He exceeded what any husband would do, he even washed the soiled nappies; he was fantastic.

You don't know what to do really. We just sort of sat there. The GP said the next thing was that someone would have to come over from the coroner's office. We rang my parents and told them what had happened, and my father came at once. I didn't have much of a back-up from my mother, I think it was more than she could cope with. It hurt me very much at the time, she couldn't stomach it and went and sat in the hairdresser's that morning which I find incredible. My father was superb to us; he and Stephen seemed to think that the most important thing to do was to remove everything in the house that was connected with the baby, which they did immediately. The pram disappeared, everything went in the half hour they spent clearing everything out. I don't know now how Stephen had that kind of forethought: those things would have been such painful reminders.

They attacked everything – I suppose I was grateful, except that I hunted around for days trying to find something they had missed. I was desperate to find something, and I found quite a lot. But there is nothing to do: people think that when these things happen you're rushing around and having hysterics but you're not because you're so stunned and shocked you haven't got any hysterics to have. It comes days and days afterwards. I did cry that day but nothing like days afterwards when it finally hit me. Nobody wants to come near you because they are frightened. You sit there; what do you do? You smoke cigarettes, you drink cups of coffee, you feel ill, you feel cold. I was frozen all day. It was the middle of May and I remember feeling violently cold.

The next thing that happened was that a man and a policeman arrived at the door; I remember that in ridiculous detail. By this time Lucy had been dressed and gone to a friend who rose to the occasion fantastically. We didn't tell Lucy what had happened: she was only just two, she was a baby herself. The policeman horrified me: I have this old-fashioned idea that policemen in ordinary houses are in some way pointing the finger. He had a man from the coroner's office and a funeral director with him, and we had to sit and go over what had happened the previous night, which was just the normal baby routine. The funeral director's assistant during this time had disappeared: I was standing in the sitting room and the man from the coroner's office started to talk to me in a quite deliberate manner as if to avert my attention from the window. By doing so he made me look out of the window of course, and I saw a metal box being taken down my drive and being put in the boot of his car. I flipped. I got hysterical. It was so awful. By then we had put him back up in his room because we didn't think, rightly or wrongly, that Lucy should see him. I didn't know what to do with him – I just put some clean sheets out. I thought if they were going to take him away I ought to put clean sheets out: you do such stupid things, don't you?

After his body had been taken away they asked us if we wanted his clothes and did we want him buried or cremated. You feed a perfectly normal baby at ten thirty one night and the following morning by ten o'clock you are being asked whether you want him buried or cremated. I think it's more than you can cope with. It was so awful when they took him away in those circumstances – nobody had dreamt of it happening. We chose to have him buried, which I regret sorely now because we have moved away and the grave is neglected, which upsets me. Even though it is a very short walk from our parents' home, it's something they're not prepared to do anything about and we had him buried there with that in mind because we knew we would be moving around. I go to my parents once a year but I can't bear it more often than that. I'll force myself to go up to the churchyard, but it upsets me terribly – not the fact that he is buried there, but that it looks so awful. Originally I used to go there every day just to be near him: there were always flowers there. As time went by I went less often – it got to being every week, but nonetheless it was looked after and it looked as if somebody cared. We couldn't afford a headstone at the time and there still isn't one because we have got to the stage now of not communicating about it. When we first moved away I used to send my mother money to buy flowers on his birthday and for Christmas, but now it all seems rather pointless – it isn't going to achieve anything, and it doesn't.

I understand how my husband feels; I don't agree with how he feels but I understand his way of thinking. He thinks that I feel too deeply about it all and that I get too upset about it even now, which he finds hard to understand after seven years. So we don't talk about it now and consequently I don't get upset, and the longer one doesn't talk about something the more difficult it is to talk about. I think if he were to start talking about it now I'd be so stunned I probably wouldn't be able to talk about it to him! He thinks there's little point in dwelling on it. What's happened has happened and is a part of the past. We have coped with it and we have got our two daughters so we are very fortunate. Nothing is going to bring him back, which is quite true, but Stephen has put him in the past and yet he is part of our present as well. I feel I need to bring him back into being: it's time I told Lucy, she is able to understand now.

At the time I had had so little experience of death that I remember feeling unable to cope. I had lost a very close girl-friend just before – we were expecting babies at the same time. She had a Thomas but died having him. He was her fourth child. I couldn't take in her death either, even now I can't take them both in because it is just so awful: her dying and leaving her poor little baby – really and truly if one is rational about it, her husband had quite enough to cope with without another baby on his plate; and our baby dying that Stephen wanted: it seems such a stupid waste, the whole thing is so ridiculous.

I think I went through every feeling there is in the first six months: I was angry, I was bitter at everyone, people's reactions got on top of me, they said stupid things that made me furious. As they don't know how to describe a cot death, there isn't an official name for it. They call it virus pneumonia so that is what is on the death certificate. We lived in a fairly small village and these things get around and someone said to me one day, 'You have to keep babies warm': I was so angry. Other people turned their backs and didn't want to talk to me. I did have some very good friends who were superb, absolutely fantastic. Nonetheless, our immediate friends were so shocked and upset that they didn't know how to approach us. People in the village certainly didn't know how to and they kept out of our way rather than talk to us about it, which didn't help. I went into the village shop and I felt I wanted to scream at them, 'For God's sake talk to me someone, somebody mention it. Why doesn't someone say something to me?' Everybody knew everybody and you jolly well knew that you were being talked about. It bugs me to this day: the whole thing has been shelved as though it had never happened: forgotten, gone. It was a nasty thing that we must put out of our minds.

My parents never talk about it although my mother, who is an extremely tactless person and has a habit of saying very hurtful things, said to me a year ago, 'Don't you ever imagine the three of them, one, two, three?' and I thought to myself, 'You stupid woman, of course I do. I would be an idiot if I didn't.' I don't want to talk to my mother about it, and my father is rather bound up in his own grief. Unfortunately, he is one of those men who desperately wanted boys: my sister had two girls and he was over the moon when I had a son. He is boy-mad and had great ambitions for his grandson and he took it extremely badly. He would suffer very quietly and get so bottled up about it that he would be quite difficult to communicate with. He did cry – when he first came over he cried; I have never seen my father cry before.

My husband talked to me and comforted me and let me cry and he hasn't suppressed me in any way. He doesn't now, either. It's just that he said he wouldn't keep coming to the grave with me, that it wasn't doing me any good, in fact it was making me ill. He said it with the best of intentions, because time wasn't helping me, I was getting worse in fact. He said that no amount of flowers or coming and standing by the grave is going to bring him back, and there is some sense in that way of thinking. But a man probably thinks differently anyway.

I had post-natal depression thrown in with all this as well which was the finishing touch, and the other ghastly thing was that I had to go and have a post-natal check-up. You have got no baby with you but you have got to go and be messed about with. It was traumatic. I suppose we kept on talking about it for a couple of years – I used to mention it and burst into tears on anniversaries, but I don't do that any more. Stephen has never told me not to talk about it, but his attitude to death is very different to mine. Mine is rather dramatic and emotional, his is that there's no good dwelling

27

on it, it's gone, it's finished, it's final. To me, he still exists in my mind but I feel rather isolated in this because it's only in my mind and not in anybody else's. I would like to keep him fresh in our minds, and that's where it would help to share him with the girls. I've had three children and he is a part of my family. They would probably love to know that they have a brother. When Lucy was little she used to come to the grave with me, but she never knew who it was. She apparently has no memory of it. I don't know whether it's a little part of her mind that's shut it out – we certainly did say to her at the time that he'd gone away and that we didn't want him to but we had to put up with it. She asked where he was and where the pram was – she adored the pram and loved to help push it. My parents bought her a large doll's pram which stopped the questioning instantly. I got very protective over her, I got so anxious about everything she did, and that went on for several years.

Our GP said that the best thing to do was to become pregnant straight away and since he had been through the same thing we took his advice. Three months later I was pregnant again and I had a miscarriage. I had a most peculiar reaction towards it: I didn't want it anyway, I'd convinced myself that it wasn't really a baby I was expecting and that I would get used to it as time went by. I couldn't understand myself. I got roped into hospital again when I lost it and I hated it: they put 'Abortion' over my bed which I thought was appalling. I discharged myself feeling really ill – I looked ghastly and I felt ghastly. Then three months later I was pregnant again with Sophie.

When she was born they tried to persuade me to feed her myself, but I wouldn't. I had fed Thomas to start with but I stopped several weeks before he died. But there was no way I was going to feed Sophie. I hadn't got a name for her, I didn't know what to call her, it was just as if it wasn't really me that had had her. It was weird. Stephen wanted the name Sophie so that was fine, and I thought she was quite sweet. But when I got home with her I got in such a panic – the same house, and we used to bump into each other going up and down stairs when we had been creeping into her room to make sure she was all right. I thought it was only me doing it and he thought it was only him doing it and in fact it was both of us. It was ridiculous, I used to stand there and give her a little poke to make her move.

She was a non-event as far as my family were concerned. My mother came into the hospital and said, 'Are you a bit disappointed that you haven't had another boy?', upon which my husband had to go out of the room. His very words were that if he hadn't gone out he would have hit her. People didn't quite know what to say to me afterwards, whether to say, 'Isn't it super you've had a girl?' or, 'Would you have liked a boy?' I made a point of saying that I didn't want a boy. I desperately didn't want a boy. I felt if I had a boy and it looked like him, I would go bananas. I didn't want a replacement. We have never thought of Sophie as that; she was her own person, most definitely. That wasn't the reason for having another baby, although I did desperately need another baby to keep myself occupied as much as anything. Lucy of course had gone back to being the only one, which I didn't want.

There is never a day goes past when I don't think of him. I used to do nothing but think of him, and I thought even when I had another baby I'd still think all day, but I didn't, I was so busy. Even now I'm often reminded of him and think of him, but it's not necessarily upsetting. I can talk about it quite rationally without crying. The reason we managed to gather ourselves together in a reasonably short time was because we had Lucy, and we couldn't make her life a misery. It doesn't matter what you do as far as other people are concerned: I am convinced that people used to think that I was hard because I did gather myself together – you could almost see people thinking, 'My goodness, the baby only died six weeks ago and there she is smiling.' People's reactions will always be critical whatever you do.

What I needed was sympathy and a listening ear, and time to cry. When it hit me most was after the first couple of weeks. My husband stayed at home for a week and for a couple of weeks people were absolutely super. I didn't have any time on my own. I didn't have time to sit and think; but inevitably that stops, and when it did I got into a terrible state. I totally and absolutely lost my religious faith, I went into a church and I had to come out. I thought, 'What a farce it all is.' But you can't go on thinking like that and since then I have grown up a bit and taken a more rational attitude towards it. I can't make up my mind whether I really believe that there is something after life. We don't go to church and we don't take the children to church. I think I need to believe in something to keep going, but for Stephen, he thinks that life finishes here. But I was angry with God, I was furious with him. I had lost my best friend and a baby in the space of four months and I couldn't see any reason for that at all. People tell me that worse things happen to other people, but as far as I was concerned everything bad was happening to me then. In the end it taught me more about life in some ways. It has taught me to value my children more than most people do – so many take them for granted because they haven't had the experience that I had. They don't think they are particularly lucky; I think I am very fortunate to have had another child afterwards when so many other things could have happened: my husband was talking about having a vasectomy at the time and mercifully hadn't had it done. I think I have calmed down as a person; I don't get so wrought up about things and I don't panic so easily.

I dreamt about Thomas constantly afterwards: it was horrid. My most frequent dream was that he was up in the loft with the basket and all the gear and it was all very silly, why would somebody put him up there? I would wake up and ask Stephen to go and fetch him. It occurred over and over again. The other one was I used to dream quite frequently how ghastly it must be under all that earth, and how cold on cold days and how wet on wet days and how nasty for him.

I feel constantly guilty, partly because I didn't feed him myself – they thought that might be a cause – and I feel terribly, passionately guilty about the previous week because I gave him no attention whatsoever. I fed him, bathed him, and changed him and shoved him off to a neighbour or a friend. I ignored his crying on several occasions that week because I was so worried about Lucy and I had so much to do. The days weren't long enough and I was constantly tired because he was waking up early in the mornings, and also because of the after-effects of the birth. It all got on top and I don't like not being able to cope. That week the whole system went haywire and I feel terribly guilty about that. One particular day during that week he screamed and screamed and screamed and I could not find out what was wrong. I lost my temper and bounded upstairs with the basket and threw it on to my bed and slammed the door. I had to get him out of earshot – Lucy was being sick at the time and the phone was ringing and so I let him lie up there and scream which I feel dreadful about now. But these things become mountainous in the mind. To me now the whole week seemed a nightmare, an absolutely ghastly nightmare.

We went to the wedding the following day; God knows how, I still don't know how. My sister wanted to cancel the wedding but I remember telling her she couldn't do it. Lucy was a bridesmaid, and we went. I can't remember it all. That was a bit of strength that was given to us, I am convinced of that. There was an inquest the following week, and then the burial – we didn't have a funeral as such, just prayers in the chapel. The vicar in the village was so kind, he was smashing to us; very aged but very sweet. I didn't want anyone to wear black, I hate black and I thought it was so appalling that people should wear black for a baby somehow. I told everyone, and my mother wore black. She is old-fashioned and wanted to have tea and cakes afterwards which nobody wanted, but when I saw her in black (I had been doing quite well up until then) I went bananas and screamed at her for being so thoughtless and wearing that awful black.

The funeral was a little hurdle overcome – I remember the feeling of disbelief as they lowered the little coffin into the ground. I had only been to one funeral before, that of my friend, but I hadn't seen the interment. So this was the first time I had ever been through the whole ritual. I didn't know what happened at funerals. I thought it was appalling. The previous day we had been over to the graveyard and there was a hole already dug and I just couldn't believe this hole, this awful hole. I knew it was his because it was so small.

I have got one very small photo of him: it was dreadful, because on the film we took of him while he was alive only one photograph came out, and in it he looks just like he did when he died. I had to put it away. We regret it so much but it doesn't change things; I wish it did. We have got nothing to hang on to, it's just gone. I kept his clothes for years, but Stephen burned the basket and all the other equipment one day while I was out. I wasn't content with that, I went down and poked in the bonfire to see what I could find. It was so stupid – you do such ridiculous things.

My mother-in-law was wonderful; she sent us meals over every day which was superb because we didn't want to think about food or prepare a meal, and these food parcels kept appearing. She also offered to buy us another house if we couldn't stand living there: her offers of help were very practical. I did find his room very painful. That was one of the reasons that we did eventually move, we wanted a fresh start but it took us time to realise that. She also gave me a holiday in the summer and she was very sympathetic about Thomas; she was very sweet but it's not quite the same as your own mother somehow.

Now we lead perfectly normal lives, nothing seems out of the ordinary because it has all been shelved. But not by me, it's still very much alive in my mind. I think we ought to say something about it to the girls, because in a funny way I want them to love him too. It will teach them that people suffer and people die. They are old enough to understand. I got to the point where I tried writing about it – to help other people as much as myself and I got up to the part where I first saw him dead, and I couldn't bear to write it down, I can talk about it but I can't write it down. I do sometimes wonder, 'Did it all happen to me?' It all seems like a bad dream.

Several years ago nobody knew what a cot death was. People now are more willing to talk about it and are more forthcoming; they reckon it's 2000 babies a year and that's a lot of babies. People are writing articles about it and it's not getting shovelled under the carpet quite as much as it was. The guilt part of it is so awful; people asked me if he'd suffocated or if he'd turned over in his sleep or if he'd had a cold – and it was endless, they were trying to find reasons. But you can't dismiss the whole idea of people thinking how strange it all is. Somebody said to me when she heard I'd had a cot death, 'I had a miscarriage too.' I thought, 'Hold your cool, girl. God, I have lost a baby and I have had a miscarriage and it's not the same thing.' My miscarriage meant nothing to me, it wasn't a baby. But having lost a baby, a real baby whom I'd looked after, who was a person, you can't compare that with losing masses and masses of blood. How different the loss is: I think it's terrible to confuse them. I'll never get over it: I shall just get used to it.

4

MARY AND GAVIN:
their two-year-old daughter

Mary and Gavin live in south London; she is thirty-three and he thirty-eight. Gavin works in a children's assessment centre and Mary is a telephonist and receptionist. They both love children and their warmth and obvious desire for a family make them seem ideally suited to parenthood. Their story is heart-rending: after having had two miscarriages, Mary eventually became pregnant again. Just over two years ago she gave birth to a daughter with Down's syndrome, Anna. After the initial shock, they had only to discover that she also had Hirschsprung's disease, which was causing a gut obstruction. However, she had a successful operation and seemed to be making normal progress. But when she was two she developed measles and it was then discovered that she was acutely ill with incurable leukaemia; two months later she died. Because of the exceptional domiciliary care offered by the doctors from the hospital, Anna was able to die at home, nursed by her parents. Four months later Mary unwillingly returned to work, and she explained how, seven months after Anna's death, she was going through her worst time yet.

Grief fills the room up of my absent child,
Lies in his bed, walks up and down with me,
Puts on his pretty looks, repeats his words,

34

**Remembers me of all his gracious parts,
Stuffs out the vacant garments with his form; ...**

Shakespeare: *King John*

Mary: I do want children and I've got to the point now where I'd like children around me, and going back to work is like going back a few years. I feel when this year's over with – although you shouldn't wish your life away – I'll be able to start afresh.

Still, it is early days. At first, although I knew what had happened, I was anaesthetised for ages. I think I'm going through my worst time now. At the time, we had to nurse Anna and it was absolutely essential that we kept our feet on the ground. The two doctors were fantastic – we kept saying to them, 'You've been wonderful,' but I don't think they realised how marvellous they were. They couldn't really do anything for Anna, so I think they thought to themselves that the best way to help was to support us while we were looking after Anna at home. They were very truthful, very honest, and always there. I said to Gavin at one point, 'I don't think they get any sleep.' We were ringing them up in the middle of the night towards the end and they were marvellous. They left us with something we'll never lose. Anna was happy at home. Right towards the end she used to look around her own room and I know she was glad to be there. She'd been in hospital so much and she always used to know when she was there; you wouldn't think a two-year-old would be so sensitive.

She was a really fantastic kid. She was always ready to laugh. My God, with what she went through, I wouldn't be ready to laugh. Gavin and I really admired her. It sounds silly but she was great. She used to stay in hospital for about a week at the stage when she got tummy blockages, and when we used to bring her home her eyes used to go all round and she used to wriggle her bottom – 'Ooh, I'm home.' I think the saving grace was that she was able to die at home. We had exceptional care and we were so grateful, because without that we wouldn't have been able to do what we did for Anna.

It enabled us to do what we wanted to do for her and if we hadn't had them I don't know what we would have done. Towards the end it was ever so frightening – she used to start scratching her face if she got anxious, as if she knew something was up. We realise now she was going into heart failure and of course it was frightening to watch.

Gavin: We didn't know what to expect.

Mary: It's terrible, you've got nothing left when a little child that age dies.

Gavin: It was as if Anna knew as well. It helped her no end to die at home. She didn't like hospitals at all towards the end – she'd had so many dealings with them. The last time she was in hospital she was under very heavy sedation, but she refused to go to sleep. We asked if we could take her out in the car, and we had to promise to bring her back again.

Mary: She went to sleep in the car and we tiptoed back into the hospital, but as soon as we got back into that ward, she woke up. It was as if to say, 'For goodness' sake will you take me home.' The doctor said, 'Well, I've given her so much sedation that I can't give her any more,' so we brought her home and put her in her cot. She took one look around and went straight to sleep. That's when the treatment changed; from that time on we nursed her at home. She had a cot down here in the sitting room; it must have been a lovely feeling for her.

Gavin: We took her to visit my Mum at the coast for a change of scenery a few days after they told us that she had leukaemia and that they couldn't cure her. I remember taking her into my Mum's room and she gave a little grunt of disapproval as if she was thinking, 'I don't know where I am, where are we?' She was a bit afraid, I think.

Mary: When she was at home and indoors she knew she was safe. She relaxed a lot more. She had her birthday party at home and it was really fantastic, she relaxed so much. She had such a good time because the party was in her house and not in hospital. That was a really super day.

She had always been ill, right from birth, but we were just managing to get used to it. The first year of life wasn't too bad, really – we had to look after her when she had the colostomy but it didn't hold her progress back. She came on in leaps and bounds. It didn't really stop her from doing anything. It was when the colostomy was reversed that all the trouble started.

Gavin: It was then that she got her hate of hospitals. She caught gastro-enteritis and she was ever so poorly. They said we nearly lost her then. She'd had so many injections and she got very miserable. On top of the operation, she'd had enough of it. She was there for nearly two months and that's a long time.

Mary: We had to dilate her once a week when she got home, and she absolutely hated it. We used to have these gloves to do it with and you wouldn't think that she would know, but once when she was perfectly well again she was sitting in the kitchen playing, and I put some rubber gloves on to do some washing up and she really howled. I went to pieces. I thought, 'That poor little baby, she knows.' What with all the medicines and needles she was cheesed off.

We were just about getting over that when we were hit with the shock of when they told us that she was going to die of leukaemia. She had been coming on so well. She was virtually normal really, she was fantastic, having had such a bad start. She had so much patience.

Gavin: She was no trouble whatsoever. We're biased I suppose, but she was good here. She gave us about five bad nights in all, in two years.

Mary: She was very good. Even though she was a mongol, she was bright and alert. I'm glad we had that. I think if she'd been ill from birth we wouldn't have had any of that. But she had some good times, she really did. I think because she was a mongol I spent more of my time with her. When she was born and I was told, I thought, 'Oh dear, how awful,' and then I thought, 'OK so she's a mongol but she's going to be the best one that there is.' We used to play all the time, and I'm glad now that I spent so much time with her: we went swimming, she had a lot of friends and there wasn't much we didn't do. She really had a good time.

Immediately after they told us that she would die of leukaemia it just seemed unreal. I couldn't really believe it.

The doctor got a bit anxious and said, 'You do realise what's happening, don't you?', and I said, 'Yes, I do.' I nursed Anna from birth and I was used to nursing her and I thought, 'Well, this is the only thing that I've got left, so I've really got to keep a grip on myself.' I can't really remember what I thought, I just felt I had to nurse her, that it was the last thing that I could do for her.

Gavin was absolutely marvellous; he gave me a lot of support. If I'd been told the news and Anna hadn't been ill before, this would have been my first nursing job and I don't know how I would have reacted. But the nursing part of it wasn't new to me. I think I felt completely numb. I feel worse now – it's more painful now.

When it got to the end I was simply so concerned that Anna didn't suffer. I thought, 'If she goes on and on, the leukaemia is going to take over really badly.' I didn't know too much about leukaemia – just that there are different sorts and it reacts in different ways. I was terrified that she was going to suffer in any way and towards the end I thought, 'Please let her go.' In the end it was a bit of a relief when she did die, because we were so terrified that she was going to be hurt. She'd suffered long enough and enough was enough. And we were complete nervous wrecks.

Gavin: When she died, it was so peaceful. It was overwhelming, the feeling, it really was.

Mary: We passed that feeling of death, in a way; we were so thankful that it was peaceful. She just went to sleep, literally, and she was with Gavin. He was holding her and it couldn't have been better. So we've got that. When you look back on that, it's marvellous to be left with because you haven't got much left to hold on to. She was really brave – she really helped *us*.

Gavin: It was always she who helped us more than anything. We hoped that she might have a little more time, and we still didn't put everything down to leukaemia. She was cutting some teeth and we thought if we could get her over that she'd have a bit more time. About three days before she died, we'd gone out for a drink and she was sitting with us on the common eating crisps. If she'd stayed in hospital she would never have had that. It was a beautiful sunny day. That was Saturday and she died on the Tuesday.

Mary: We used to take her out in her pram – it was loaded up with bottles and chocolate and nappies and medicine just so that we could walk for miles. She used to love it; it was really marvellous that we could do that. If she had been in hospital she wouldn't have had any of that. It pleased us that we could do so much for her.

Gavin: When she died it was like a numbness. I still don't believe it now, it's still unreal. Some days it really hits me and upsets me quite a bit. Suddenly something outstanding hits me and then I realise: but I still can't believe that she's gone. I feel a great need of her – I feel I want to pick her up and cuddle her, hold her. I feel an ache. Sometimes I feel very very angry, I want to release my anger in some way, but I can't. The frustration wells up inside and I feel I want to smash something. I don't know what to do about it, although it's getting less and less now. When I go and see her at the cemetery I ask, 'Why? Why?' There's a sort of futility about it, I just don't understand why. But it does help to go and see her at the cemetery: I feel as if I'm closer to her.

Mary: For me, that depends on the weather. If it's a nice bright sunny day, it's lovely to go there and take some flowers. But when it's miserable and cold I just want to pick her up and bring her in here in the warm. We're quite lucky though really because it's so lovely and peaceful over there; it must be awful for people to go to graves when they're all untidy and uncared for. You walk in through the gates and it's kept so lovely: it's small, it's another world, it's peaceful.

Gavin: It means a lot. We're not religious people, we don't believe she's there, really, it's more out of love that we go.

Mary: You can take flowers, and it's a kind of contact still.

Gavin: I remember how marvellous we felt when we first went over to find a place for her. I think the chap who runs the cemetery understood how we felt – she was still a part of us then. That was a nice period, those few days afterwards, but that's all disappeared since. We didn't feel then that we'd lost her.

Mary: I feel worse now than I did at the beginning. I get

more upset, I cry more now. Sometimes at work it's a terrible strain because I have to be all bright and cheerful. It takes up every ounce of energy and I think, 'Oh, God, I can't keep this up.' But it does me good because I have to make the effort or else I'd never go out of the house – but it does leave me drained. We're absolutely exhausted most of the time but I suppose it's just a phase you go through.

I forget things terribly, especially at work. Sometimes I don't know how I manage to get by. I have to write everything down, otherwise I'm lost. I just about manage to go through the motions and I get through by the skin of my teeth, but in a way I feel I'm not really there – because I don't want to be there. It's awful for Gavin because he's the breadwinner; it doesn't really matter if I can't cope.

Gavin: I never bring it to mind at work; if things crop up like a record on the radio that she liked, it helps that I can get involved in the job and forget about things. It hits me more later, when I come home and walk back into where she belonged. I'm quite an emotional person and I find it hard to hide my feelings in front of Mary; if I get upset it upsets her. It's an awful fight inside trying not to get upset.

Mary: It's in for the day when you're both upset, it's awful. I know crying is a form of release and we get over it quite quickly. You think, 'Oh good, it'll go,' yet you can feel it coming over you like a big black cloud. We can talk to each other about it but he's so emotional and you both know how you feel, so you haven't really got to say anything. I've got this terrible need to talk about her all the time, and I've got this friend who has been fantastic. She's a very understanding person and I've just talked and talked and I've talked it out of my system. I only hope that one day I can help somebody like that. She's just listened, and if she has said anything, it's been the right thing. I depend on her quite heavily. I don't know how people manage if they can't talk about it.

With other people, I've noticed that they back off a bit, they don't want to talk about it. I suppose they're frightened you're going to get upset. I think it's a bit selfish – they're not aware of your need to talk. I wonder if I've ever been like that with anyone. They backed off too when they heard that

Anna was a mongol. I can remember saying at the time, 'I will always put myself out in future and say something to people.' It's changed both of us in that respect: it's changed our outlook. It can make you feel so isolated if people turn the other way. We realise that now we've experienced it.

Gavin: It's showed me that death and grief are things you have to face. They should be brought more into everyday life and be accepted. It's there, all the time, and we tend to push it away. We feel that perhaps she's somewhere else – I don't know how people cope if they don't have that belief.

Mary: It's made me think more about religion, rather than turning me against it. I want to look into it more and it's made me think about it.

Gavin: The letters we had afterwards meant a lot to me. They made me very proud of Anna.

Mary: When we had Anna buried we were absolutely amazed at how many people there were there. We really felt she must have meant something to those people. She'd proved herself and we felt really proud of her, especially being a mongol. She was a real person and the tribute from all those people helped enormously. We were both very moved, and all the flowers were very comforting. People were very kind – their letters and cards were sweet.

We've got quite a few photos of her and she was a pretty little baby. It was important to me that she looked pretty, being a mongol. She had gorgeous hair. We've got lots of cine film but we haven't been able to look at it yet – it's too soon and I'm not strong enough.

Gavin: I remember the awful feeling I had when we were told that she was dying – we wanted to do even more for her. The first few days afterwards I think she was aware of how strangely we were acting.

Mary: I kept picking her up and cuddling her.

Gavin: She must have thought, 'What's going on?', because we were round her every couple of minutes. We realised that that couldn't go on. I felt let down by the doctors at this stage because they were afraid of telling us how long she had got. Perhaps they couldn't tell us when it was going to be, but if I'd had some sort of idea, I could have done more for her.

41

Mary: I honestly don't think that they could tell. The doctor said to me, 'Enjoy every day that comes.'

Gavin: Because I didn't have a definite date I went along the lines that she'd go on for ever. I wouldn't admit to myself that it was going to happen. If they'd said a couple of months, or six months, or whatever, it would have helped me in the way that I reacted. I regret now that we said we'd carry on as normal: I spent even less time with her than I would have done. I'd have tried not to make it obvious to her but I would have involved myself that little bit more with her. That's my only regret. I'm a bit envious of Mary really, she spent so much time with her.

Mary: I think it's just a reaction: you had more time at home with her than most fathers do. You were often playing with her in the morning while I was still in bed.

Gavin: There was one terrible thing that happened – really hurtful. We had one beautiful day on the coast just after we'd been told about the leukaemia, and she had a smashing time. We took what we thought would be lovely photographs of her and we took them in to be developed. They messed them up on us, they all got destroyed. We didn't get one; and the birthday party was on that reel, too. We couldn't believe it. I can hardly talk about it. I felt awful actually, taking pictures of her knowing that she was about to die. It didn't seem right, it was morbid in a way. It wasn't natural.

We both find that we're very selfish as regards our own feelings. We've always shared everything ever since we've been married, but I can't help Mary and she can't really help me. We have to cope for ourselves. It's like being an outsider – you know how they feel and you try to help but you can't. It's something we can't share at the moment.

Mary: There's nothing really we can do for each other. I know how you feel and there's nothing I can do to talk you out of it. There isn't an answer to it – it's there and that's it. That's where I've been very lucky with my friend. She's seen me through a bad time in a way that nobody else, even your nearest and dearest, could. I had her on the end of the telephone and she was a safety valve. I can't imagine what it must be like to be alone – I can understand people dying of a broken heart now.

It's quite physical, the way it affects you. The aching. Good job you don't feel like it every day – there are days when you wake up and you know it's not going to be too bad, and that gets you through. If you felt that terrible all the time I don't think you would. We both had a few sleeping tablets after Anna died, but neither of us have needed any other pills. I was sleeping so soundly – as soon as my head hit the pillow, I was off. I sleep like a rock: keeping myself occupied during the day and trying to keep that depression off is so exhausting that there's no problem. I couldn't bear it if I had insomnia; if I go to bed a bit early, and lie there, sometimes the whole feeling of what's happened comes over me and it's unbearable.

Gavin: You do get more upset now than you ever did. I was surprised at how marvellous you were at the beginning. I knew you were very upset inside, but you only got really low a couple of months ago.

Mary: It was because I was having to nurse her. We had to keep our feet on the ground, and we had all that support which made things easier. It gave me something to do *for* her. She didn't have too much pain – I honestly think her teeth gave her the most discomfort.

It all happens when it happens. On top of two miscarriages, all Anna's problems. It wasn't just being a mongol – that was awful to start with, naturally – but everything else as well. I'd really have to know what was what before I went in for another baby. It's frightening to think of it happening all over again. I don't honestly think I could take it. I've taken so much and managed to keep sane but I don't think I could take any more. It was only because Anna didn't suffer that I managed to take this much. Had she been in any sort of pain I don't feel I would be the person I am today quite frankly. If I'd seen her in a lot of distress I'd have cracked up.

When I was pregnant I knew something was wrong. People thought I was neurotic but I thought she would be a mongol. I felt awful from start to finish and that's not normal for a healthy specimen like me. If we decided to go ahead and have another baby, we could have tests to detect any chromosome deficiencies, but to me that seems like rejecting Anna.

She was Anna, she was a baby, she was a mongol but she never let us down in any way. She was as bright as a button.

Gavin: When she was very poorly at the beginning, we obviously wanted the worst to happen, because of what we'd been told. But she certainly changed our way of thinking.

Mary: Oh, yes. She was ours. We were horrified when she was born, let's face it. Our world fell apart. But she was ours and you can't let somebody down when they need you the most. No way would we have rejected her. She was so poorly, and it was such a shock, and if anything had happened then we would have accepted it as fate, that it was meant to be. But looking back now, we wouldn't have had our two years with Anna.

Gavin: It depends too on what you think of when you think of mongolism. My picture was of a kid with his head on one side and his tongue hanging out. To me Anna was a little girl, nothing else. Some of the little mongols we've met are beautiful, perfectly lovely little kids. They're just happy, beautiful, lovely people with lovely temperaments. Anna never complained of anything she had.

Mary: She was amazing. Her play was very imaginative and she had a great sense of humour. She was really a little person. She used to love her dollies and her teddies, and she used to like to go swimming.

Gavin: That was another hurtful thing, really, the fact that we had accepted her mongolism and we were in fact looking forward to the challenge. To us she had a future, and then that was taken away.

Mary: When somebody comes and says, 'I'm afraid your child will be mentally handicapped,' no-one's going to accept it with a smile – they're maniacs if they do. But she did have a future as far as we were concerned and we had plans for her.

Gavin: We were looking forward to the future. It was even more exciting than a normal child actually, because we met so many nice people through her. That's what made it all seem so useless really. I don't understand that side of it at all. She had everything going for her, she was a terrific looking kid and she had this lovely temperament. We took her every-where and she was accepted by everyone. In fact she was an advertisement for mongolism; that's the way I always looked at her.

Mary: I realise now that I've got an awful lot of patience that I didn't realise I had before. Once this year's over with I hope that things will sort themselves out. We feel as if it's out of our hands. We're floating along waiting for things to happen.

Gavin: We can't make any concrete plans. We feel that we're just managing to hold our own. We need to be led into decisions and situations, we can't actually do it ourselves. We haven't really accepted it yet. If we find something of Anna's we can't throw it away. Everything of hers is upstairs. If I put my hand down the side of a chair and find one of her little slides, I have to keep it. But we don't want to make the place a shrine to her.

Mary: At first I used to be able to go into her room, but now I can't. I get too upset. We've left her teddy and her little plaque on the door and that doesn't upset me. It's walking in that is dreadful.

Gavin: We latch on to anything to do with bereavement now. On a radio programme the other day somebody said it took them six months before they could part with the clothes. But we couldn't do that yet – and I suppose I'm thinking along the lines unconsciously that if we have any more children, they can have all this. It's taught us so much about death. I know I could cope now with a situation involving death. It wasn't an awful experience at all with Anna. There was nothing horrific about it. I remember your mum coming through the door and we hadn't covered Anna over, and she gasped – I hadn't realised what it must be like for someone who hadn't been there, coming in off the street. But she was all right after a little while and she didn't recoil. I said, 'Come on, you can see her, pick her up. It's Anna and she's dead.'

Mary: We didn't have time to think about other people, we were too busy thinking about ourselves. We don't realise what they must have been through. Poor Mum was worried about Gavin and me and upset about Anna. It must have been awful for her. Anna only stayed in the house a few hours after she died. I wanted to have her in the house longer.

Gavin: I thought it might be too upsetting. It was all so matter-of-fact afterwards – not knowing what to do; and the doctor wasn't too sure, she'd only ever done it through the hospital. So it was strange to all of us. I had to make the arrangements that day without thinking.

Mary: I can't remember exactly how I felt, my mind's a complete blank. I remember things happening but I can't remember how I felt. In retrospect I would have liked to have done everything myself: I don't know what they do but I wish I'd laid her out. It didn't seem right to have outsiders doing it. I didn't want anybody else to touch her at all, it's so personal. That is a terrible regret. To take her away like that was awful. I can remember running upstairs when they did, but I can't remember anything else.

Gavin: We were all so close when she actually died. We looked at Anna and it was overwhelming. We just kept saying, 'Thank you, thank you,' and cuddling her. We were so grateful to her. It was so peaceful. It was partly relief: we knew that it was going to happen and we wanted it to happen in the end, for her sake as well as for ours. We knew there would be no more suffering – that's how we felt as she took her last breath. That stayed with me for a long while – I think that I'm coming out of it now that I've realised what happened. It's hard to explain, but I get this terrible pain, that I've lost her. It's going to take a little while to come to terms with that. People say, 'Give it time,' but I think that time makes it more real, rather than healing. Time will change things, probably. It's always going to be with me, it will always be there. Time seems to make it more final to me. I'm still mourning her and until I come out of this tunnel at the other end I'll feel like that.

But we were so grateful that everything had gone right, that it was peaceful, that the cemetery was lovely – it was a nice day and the person there was nice. It must be dreadful if those things go wrong when you're distressed like that. But everybody's been exceptionally kind to us over there – they've looked after her grave beautifully.

Mary: Even the flowers on the grave – when we went back the day after the funeral they'd arranged them beautifully. It was really sweet. We took some photos of it; I didn't think I'd be able to do that, but Mum bought her a big teddy bear and he was put in among the flowers at her head.

Gavin: She had lots of little posies and sprays; they were so beautiful – there was nothing morbid about them. The hearse looked lovely. I think that flowers can have an extraordinary impact. We thought for a long time that we weren't going to have any flowers.

Mary: I don't understand people now who say 'No flowers'. They looked lovely when they all came in. It's a shame to miss that; they were every colour under the sun. And one doctor brought a flower arrangement all in white and said, 'This is for indoors,' which was so nice of her. We really appreciated it, because flowers can help so much.

Gavin: It's amazing, but we've found that since as well. I like to see flowers growing now, they mean something that they never meant before. I never took any interest in the garden until now.

Mary: All our memories are nice memories and that's something to be left with, isn't it? We were certainly very lucky from that point of view. All the rituals worked properly for us and we really appreciated the letters. We read some of them over and over again. It was really kind of people because it must be very difficult, but it's worth the effort to write to people because it does make a big difference. I hope I could write somebody a letter in those circumstances – I wouldn't have known whether to or not, before. It's that little bit of reaching out to try and help that counts – and even if you can't help, the gesture helps.

5

BARBARA AND COLIN:
their twelve-year-old son

Barbara and Colin live in a quiet street in a small market town. She is forty-five and works in a shop; he is forty-eight and works as an inspector for the Post Office. Fifteen months ago their elder son Keith, then twelve, developed a brain tumour without warning and he died five months later after weeks of hospitalisation and treatment. Keith's younger brother, Ray, who was eighteen months younger than his brother, is their only remaining child. It is a close-knit, warm family unit with both grannies and many cousins living nearby, in a friendly and neighbourly community.

To everything there is a season, and a time to every purpose under the heaven: a time to be born, and a time to die; a time to plant, and a time to pluck up that which is planted ... A time to weep, and a time to laugh; a time to mourn, and a time to dance.

Ecclesiastes, 3, i–vi

Keith died of a tumour on the brain: he was one of the fittest children you could ever find. He was very slim, very tall, he was the image of my husband. He had big beautiful mellow eyes which got him away with an awful lot; to me naturally he was a lovely boy, but he was also to all people who knew him. Since he has died I have had so many people say what a lovely boy he was. He had great concern for old people: he was brought up with my mother here, because when he was ten years old my father died suddenly and my mother came to live nearby. When Ray was two weeks old my father-in-law dropped dead, so their other granny is nearby too. So Keith was always brought up with his grannies, and when they didn't know what to do in the holidays and it was wet weather, they used to go out the back and chop wood for the old folk and deliver it. He was a tomboy, he was a terror, he was a real boy: he couldn't bear anything cissy or girlish. When I went in to kiss him goodnight it had to be on his forehead. Often he'd sit and slide up beside me on the settee and I would put my arm around him and that was all right. To us, naturally, he was very special, but I think he was special to a lot of other people too.

The week before he was taken ill, he went down the town to buy some flowers for me for Mothering Sunday, with Ray and my aunt, and she bought him some coke and he had some crisps. On the way back he said, 'Could you stop the car, I feel sick,' and he was sick. We just assumed it was either the coke or the crisps and nothing more. The next Wednesday we were driving back from school and he said he wanted to be sick again. When I got to work the next morning I was talking to a girl about it and she said, 'Oh, don't you take any notice of it dear, it's all a part of growing up,' and I had noticed Keith develop very quickly from the Christmas to the March. The next Saturday he was very, very sick, and again we didn't pay much attention because Ray had been sick, and the children on the estate had been sick, so naturally I assumed it was a virus going around. He didn't get a lot better so our doctor gave him penicillin thinking he'd got the virus just that bit worse. Then he started to dribble out of the side of his mouth and he kept on about that: 'Oh what's this, Mum?', because he was a very fastidious boy: his clothes, himself, and everything he did had to be perfect; if it wasn't perfect he didn't want to know. He made models beautifully: I have had them down under the shelves ever since he died. He put them there and they have been there ever since.

We took him down the town on that Saturday, parked the car, went down the street and he was walking like a drunk. My husband said, 'Keith, walk properly, you're nearly thirteen, come on or it's back in the car.' We thought he was mucking about, but he said, 'My legs won't go, Dad.' Anyway we didn't take much notice and we went off and did our shopping. On the Sunday evening my husband took them up the fields with the dog and they weren't gone five minutes before they came back. My husband came into the bathroom where I was having a bath and said, 'You'll have to call the doctor in the morning,' and I said, 'Why?' and he said, 'I literally had to carry him back, he is like an old man.' The doctor saw him and examined him and did some tests on him and I must say that he was very, very thorough. We have had an awful lot of help from him and his wife, they have been very good, as has everyone. People have been wonderful. There is a lot of bad in the world but there is also a lot of good, and since Keith died I've only found the good side.

We took him over to the hospital and they thought it was meningitis, at which I nearly keeled over because I'd had a perfectly normal, healthy child. He would come in from school, grab his bike, and he'd be off down to the pool or to see one of his mates. He was just everything a boy should be: he was bright at school, he'd done very well and he was a very good athlete. I think we could have got more out of him with his work, because he was always thinking of what he was going to do next, but he was a thoroughly ordinary lovely boy – naturally I think so because I'm his mother.

The day he was buried, the church was full and they were standing in the back. I can't remember much about it; I can remember the minister saying, 'Now Barbara and Colin and Ray have got to start a new life without Keith,' and I remember thinking, 'What sort of a life?' But I think with the love of neighbours and friends and people you work with, you are supported and you do cope somehow. My husband's workmates have been fantastic. We got our money all right when we had to be away with Keith in the hospital; and there was an envelope on the table from them when we got back, with £50 in it and a note saying, 'We know we can't buy Keith anything, but will you please accept this for petrol,' and the same thing happened where I work. There were offers of cars if our car broke down or if we had to stay over there; there were offers to take the old ladies because both my mother and mother-in-law are eighty. My next-door neighbour used to do the shopping and cook things and bring little snacks round for them. My cousin down the road who has three boys of her own used to see that Ray was bathed, washed and kept clean – she did all his washing and ironing and got him to bed. They are still helping, and I have got people I can talk to at anytime.

I feel I am still in contact with Keith: he is not visual but when I am in the house on my own I sit down some mornings when Ray has gone to school and I have a coffee. If I'm unsure of anything, he tells me what to do, and it's very real; people might think I'm a nut and that it's not true, but it's very true. I had got two tickets for the Chelsea Flower Show and I felt a bit guilty about asking for time off work, and it was Keith who said, 'Oh Mum, you go, you'll enjoy it.' Keith and I both shared a great love of flowers, and I think that's where he would have finished up, working with flowers and greenhouses; that's what we were hoping for. Flowers are a contact with him: I always put a red carnation on his grave, because once when we were in Spain on holiday we saw a man selling red carnations, and he ran down and bought me a bunch. They were his flower and very special. When he died, the day he was buried we had a big heart made, all of carnations, and three red roses, one for Dad, Ray and myself.

The twelve weeks we had him home were twelve fantastic weeks: he was in hospital thirty miles away for nine weeks, then we had him home for twelve. The children round here were just fantastic when I had Keith back home that time. He was very well for a while, and quite active, although he hated the wheelchair. He wouldn't go down the town in it unless he could possibly help it. He didn't know it, but a lot of his

51

school friends didn't recognise him, he had changed so much with the treatment. He had to go back to hospital at the end. To begin with the hospital told us it was either a tumour or a virus that very day that we took him in. They were in favour of it being a virus because he had no headaches and no double vision which he should have had but didn't. He was very healthy and this just came on. There was a young girl in the bed next to him who was twelve, and she died while he was there. My husband couldn't forget her, she was so beautiful; and yet she has a nineteen-year-old sister who is completely retarded and her mother had already lost a child of three. It just doesn't seem fair.

People say to me, 'Are you bitter?' but I'm definitely not bitter because I love children, and because there obviously is a reason, and we will know that reason one day. I don't feel angry, because I think God has a purpose for Keith, I think he's working for him. As a woman said to me the other day, 'Have you ever thought that Keith is probably working to make this a better world?' She said there are special children that are just on loan to you and that you are very privileged to have had them. I think there's a lot in it; and it's a positive thought. The only time I do get bitter is when I see these boys about that ruin football matches and beat up old ladies, because they were given a chance that my Keith wasn't given, and they are abusing it. But I'm not bitter about anything else: I love children too much for that. Above all I'm sure that there is a heaven, because nothing could look as beautiful as Keith did in his coffin and not be somewhere beautiful. I would have sat there all night if I could; he looked absolutely beautiful. My husband came too, and Ray. We asked him first if he wanted to go and he said yes, and I said, 'He won't be as you knew him,' but he wanted to come. When we got to the funeral parlour my husband said, 'Are you absolutely sure that you want to go in?' and he said, 'Yes, Dad.' I kept kissing him and my husband kissed him. Ray just touched him and screamed.

While he was on radium treatment he had something like 4000 shots over four weeks and he never once complained about anything. He had a lumbar puncture and he never complained. He was pretty aware of what was going on; he knew that they had put a shunt in his brain to relieve the pressure, but he didn't know he was dying. Everything was planned for next year; 'When I'm better, Mum, we'll do so-and-so.' It was all 'What I'm going to do when I'm better.' I'm convinced he didn't know he was dying; I did and my husband did, but he couldn't accept it: he could believe it but he couldn't accept it. The only person Keith wanted at the hospital was his father: they thought as one, they worked as one. When Dad was mending the car Keith was there with him; when he was stripping off wallpaper he was there; he was a real worker and they worked as one. He was always very pleased to see me and he always wanted me there, but his main concern was his dad. My husband literally willed things into him: at one point his speech went, when the radium treatment started, and he went back to our local hospital and they got him on well there thanks to my husband as much as anything.

I can't speak too highly of the hospital. We were a family and they treated us as a family. We are a family unit, the four of us, and as the boys got older we always discussed everything with them. We asked them to make suggestions and they made some very good ones. We took them abroad on holiday. The year before Keith died we went to Venice and he couldn't see enough, he was scuttling here and there and taking everything in. That was one of my happiest times, I remember the pleasure we had from that.

He was a boy who would go up to people and talk; he used to go over to the old gentleman across the road with his pieces of railway to be soldered, and I used to say, 'You're not to go over there and keep worrying him.' I asked him one day whether Keith was being a nuisance, and he said, 'Oh, no, I like him coming over here; I have a better conversation with him than with most adults.' My husband couldn't accept it while he was ill, nor could he really accept it when he died. He thinks he is being realistic, but deep down he is bitter to think that his son was taken: I don't think he ever thought he would have to take a knocking like that. We tried for two and a half years to have a baby and then Keith came along; he was over the moon, he was everything he wanted his son to be. I had a very difficult birth with Keith, he was a forceps baby, but I made my husband promise me that if I could have another one we would. Ray was very easy, and they were as one, they were like twins.

After I collected myself a bit, my main concern was for Ray; to help him over it, because for a child – he was eleven at the time – to have the first death that you encounter happen to your brother must be frightening. People have told me that at school they were as thick as thieves, although they used to fight like cat and dog here and I used to have to separate them, but that's a natural part of being brothers. Lots of people took them for twins, although he was very much an individual. I can't see that it has affected Ray to a great extent; he has put on a very brave face. He comes up to the cemetery with me and comes to church with me. He says his prayers for his brother every night. He's not that lonely at home: he has got his three cousins round the corner.

My neighbour has been absolutely wonderful. She has five sisters: I've no one, I am an only child and so is my husband. When Keith died it suddenly hit me, when I'd made the funeral arrangements, how alone I was in that respect. My husband wouldn't have anything to do with the funeral arrangements, he left it all to me to do just what I wanted. He said, 'You have your wish,' and I must say everything was absolutely faultless. I told them I wanted perfection and perfection was what I got. I sat down the night before and fear came over me: I'd got all these people coming and how was I going to prepare everything? Until then it hadn't entered my head. My neighbour came round and saw what was wrong and she said, 'You're not doing it, I'm doing the lot.' She and my cousin did everything. I thanked them and wanted to pay them but they said no: the word was no and that was that.

I noticed that down the town when it first happened, people crossed to the other side of the street if they saw me coming: people I'd known very well. They couldn't face me. But now I am getting people coming and asking me how I am. I have found the girls at work have been most helpful, because if I have wanted to talk about Keith, they have listened, and if I haven't, they have understood. Some days I'd just want to talk about him and some days I don't, I just want to keep him to myself. I can talk about him to my husband, but he's more inclined to keep him within himself. He wants him all to himself; there was a very, very special bond. I loved Keith more than life itself, but I think my husband loved him even more. It was him and Keith, Ray and me, although we were all as one, like four corners of a square.

I lived next door to my grandmother when I was a little girl. She lost a daughter of nineteen with meningitis. I had wonderful parents and I loved my mother very much, but my grandmother was always someone very special to me; I tried to think how she coped with the same situation – she was a widow and times were much harder than they are now. I was only ten when she died and I thought my world had finished. I can always remember her telling me, 'If ever you are in trouble and if ever you want anything, always turn to God and ask him for help.' She always used to say, 'Cleanliness is next to godliness; always speak your mind; always be honest and always tell the truth.' Those are the rules that I have tried to instil in my boys. I put myself in her position and wondered how she would have coped. I try to be happy now and I go around and I laugh and talk to people, but there is still that hole there that is never going to fill; it never will. But I live my life as I know Keith would have wanted me to live it; he wouldn't want me to be unhappy and miserable because he wasn't that type of boy. He was a very happy child, and those were the twelve happiest years of our life. He lived for twelve years and we must be very grateful; twelve years is a long time. No-one could ever take his place: if I were younger I would probably have another baby but there couldn't be another Keith because no-one could ever replace him.

Now I am just left with the hope that Ray will marry and perhaps one day I will be lucky enough to be a grandma, and then I will be fulfilled again. I love children and I always have, maybe because I had such a happy childhood. When I lost my father it was one of the hardest blows I have ever taken in life. I was thirty-two and it really knocked me sideways: I thought I'd never get over it. I've had quite a lot of experience of bereavement: a year before Keith died my best friend died as she was walking home from work. She said, 'See you after lunch,' and she had a stroke in the street and died. I was getting over that, and another lady took her job and I got very friendly with her and within six weeks she died.

One thing they always admired about Keith in the hospital was his sense of humour, which he gets from his dad. The consultant was very, very kind to us, he was so gentle; in my estimation he is one of the best. They were very good to us when I stayed in the hospital for three weeks while they were giving him X-rays and a brain scan. You have to live through it, but at the time you don't realise what is happening, you're numb. The night they told us what he'd got, it was just as if I'd been struck a blow on the head that I was never going to come round from. I'd heard it happened to other people but you never think it's going to happen to you. My friend's son was killed in a motorcycle accident, and I tried to think which was worse: to know as we did that it was going to happen, or to have it happen suddenly. I really can't decide, they are two completely different things. But either way the gap is there, the hole is there and you can never fill it.

My memories will help me, and the fact that I could be with Keith while he was dying, and share his dying, has left me with treasured memories. I sat with him the whole afternoon that he was dying. The doctor asked me if I wanted a nurse but I said I wanted to sit with him on my own. It was something very precious to me, something that I will always treasure. Periodically he opened his big eyes and looked at me, and I kept kissing him. I'm quite sure he knew I was there. When he died my mother's reaction was, 'Why couldn't it have been me?' and I said, 'Well, that isn't the way God works, Mum, you should know that.' My other experiences of bereavement didn't really help me cope with this one. This was quite different, much deeper. I'd experienced death before, I had seen dead people, but it was nothing like watching your own son die, nothing at all. It was a dreadful experience. I just hope that not many people have such a dreadful experience.

I don't really dream about him: I have got this kind of contact with him, although I can't see him visually. My husband can't go to church very often because he says all he can see down there is that white coffin, but I see a beautiful baby being christened and that's my picture because it's the same church. We have very conflicting views on it, my husband and I, but I respect his views and he respects mine. I still take sleeping pills, but I have taken myself off all my other tablets – valium and librium. I felt I had to do it myself so I took myself off them. To start with I couldn't go down the town on my own; I used to get inside the supermarket and if there were queues I used to feel frustrated and want to scream, 'Move, please move.' My cousin or my aunt used to take me down and then one morning I decided I'd go off on my own because I knew I'd got to do it eventually. People are very kind to you but you can't rely on other people all the time, there are things you have to do for yourself.

I have all the treasures that Keith bought me: he made me a little owl and it is the most treasured thing that I have. I'd rather lose anything than my little owl. People say that I'm doing very well, they say they don't know how I'm doing it, but it isn't really me, something else is carrying me through. I do also have my very bad days when I want him all the time. I just want to cuddle him. He wasn't a boy to be cuddled, but I feel that I want to. Just after Keith died there was a boy in the town – either he'd been there and I hadn't noticed him, or else he had recently moved in, but he was almost Keith's double. I saw him coming towards me in the street and I wanted to run and fling my arms around him and cuddle him. I knew it wasn't Keith but the likeness was there. The next time I saw him he was wearing glasses and seemed completely different. It was just that one time I had this urge to rush up to him, and it was very difficult not to. But I am quite convinced that we will all be together again one day. I still cry a lot on my bad days: I wouldn't say they get any less frequent. People say that time heals but for me it hasn't, I don't think that time will help me at all. I just miss him more and more. There are things like his birthday on New Year's Day: we used to stay up and see in the New Year and he used to have his birthday presents. My husband and I went to bed at ten o'clock this New Year's Eve – we just couldn't face the New Year and I don't think we ever will. Then there are things like his eighteenth birthday. You think of them every hour of every day. My only hope in life now is that Ray makes a good and happy marriage, but then I have got to see another boy standing up there as best man. They are all things you have got to live with. They are very hard. Birthdays are bad, and this Christmas I had a houseful of people to help me try to forget. But Keith had kept saying, 'I'll be thirteen next birthday, Mum, you will feel like an old lady, won't you? I'll be a teenager.' And of course his thirteenth birthday never came.

As regards people, they've been marvellous. I had over 200 wonderful letters, and the day after he was buried I had a lovely bouquet of flowers. People were fantastic. There is a lot of bad in the world, a lot of greed and selfishness and terrible things about, but there is just as much good if people like to seek it out. I think people should to into a ward like the neurological ward Keith was on and see the patients; then there would be none of this discontent – people would just be thankful they had got two legs to walk on to get to work and do a job.

My husband is very understanding when I have hard days of depression. He wouldn't take any pills right from the start. He said he was going to do it on his own. He sleeps very well, and wants to cope in his own way: he is a very determined man, as was Keith. Ray is now doubly precious: he always has been, naturally, there was never any more love for one than the other, but if Ray mentions sickness now I panic, although I'm getting a bit better now. I am trying to let him lead a perfectly normal ordinary life, which is only fair to him.

My cousin had some people over only this week and she was showing a film of her holidays, and on the end of it was a shot of Keith sitting on the bridge fishing. She said he was laughing his head off with his blond hair and his T-shirt on, and she said it just about finished her, because she expected to come back over here and find him. I would love to see him on cine film, but once I had seen him I would keep wanting to see him. I don't really feel that I've parted from him, I still feel that I have got him; although I can't see him visually he is still very much a part of me, and always will be. There is a very special bond between all four of us. We lived our lives to help and suit each other. When I was ill and he had been to school, the first thing he would say as he came tearing in was, 'Are you all right, Mum, how's my Mum?' He was very kind, and wonderful with old folks. I always try to wear things that I know he would like to see me in; obviously some people think that is very silly, but his taste was my husband's taste anyway, so it works quite well.

His room is as he left it. I have given all his clothes away – the social worker came one day and I sorted them out for her. She has been wonderful – she still comes and has a coffee with me most weeks and I can really talk to her. I was first introduced to her in the early days of Keith's illness, and she has become a friend. I find I enjoy work even more now: I can't speak too highly of the people I work with, they have been just fantastic. One day my husband had taken Keith to the hospital for a check-up and they were pretty sure that the tumour was coming back, and he rang me up to tell me. I collapsed in tears and one of the girls was marvellous. The manager ran me home and said, 'If you don't feel well enough tomorrow don't come in to work, we'll understand, and if there is anything at all that you want, just give us a ring.' I went back to work the week after Keith died, and in the end I could pick out two types of people: you get those who make genuine enquiries about how you are but you also get the ones who want to know a little bit so they can gossip about how they've been talking to Barbara and how ill she looks. One old lady, so I heard from somebody else, said, 'Do you know, she is back at that shop and just buried her boy.' You get that, but I am one who can shut myself off from people if I want to anyway so I don't let it worry me.

6

KATIE AND SEBASTIAN: their eighteen-year-old son

Katie is in her forties, and happily married to Sebastian who is an executive for a large company in London. They live in an East Anglian village from which he commutes to work. They had three children: Philip who is thirteen, Stephanie who is sixteen, and Martin who was eighteen when a month ago he was killed in a motorcycle crash. It was Good Friday and he was on his way back from church: they are Roman Catholics and go to Mass regularly as a family. They are a very close and loving unit. I talked to Katie in the early days of her grief, and her parting words were, 'Come back in two years time and see if I've got over it in any way.'

> Cold in the earth – and the deep snow piled above thee,
> Far, far removed, cold in the dreary grave ...
> Once drinking deep of that divine anguish,
> How could I seek the empty world again?
>
> Emily Brontë: *Remembrance*

The fact that there are other people worse off than you doesn't actually help. I think it will eventually – when it gets through. Nothing helps at the moment, nothing gets through. I am still numb: especially so on the day of the funeral, which was about fifteen days after the accident. He was in hospital for that time, in a complete coma. We thought it better to have the funeral over quickly – we wanted it on the Wednesday because it was his feast day, but they couldn't get his body ready in time. So it had to be the Thursday. It was Stephanie's birthday, so she didn't have a very good day.

I did see Martin after he died. We went to the Chapel of Rest, and it is the most beautiful act you can do. Martin was so beautiful. He lay all in white with white lace around the cuffs and neck of the robe, and small white lace flowers covering the front. There was a trace of a smile around his mouth. His hair was combed and lay in small waves. We kissed him and touched him. We prayed, and stayed with him for about forty minutes before they took him to the church. There is nothing to be afraid of and I knew that if I did not see him then for the last time on this earth, it would be too late afterwards.

The two other children are so good: they've really helped me, especially Stephanie. She was so concerned. I'm a bit worried about Philip, because he's only thirteen and it hasn't registered. It's not real to him, I don't think. He showed his grief when he was told: he always makes the tea on Saturday mornings – they've all done that – and we all climb into bed. We decided to tell him then. He cried a lot, immediately, but he didn't cry again until the evening after the funeral. I heard him crying on the stairs and I went and sat with him and just talked to him. I think it's difficult for him. Yet children are so resilient, and it's not as if he had Martin as I did, as a son. It's a different relationship and a different reaction. And of course Martin wasn't here: he was at boarding school. It was his last term of 'A' levels. He liked younger boys and Philip worshipped him, he was his hero. I think it must be a great loss to him, but he can't show it. He doesn't cry and I don't think that he can. It's rather difficult – he hasn't been to the grave yet I don't think, unless he's gone and I haven't seen him.

I do find it a great help, going to his grave. I don't go very often: twice a week perhaps. He's right there, just over the wall from here. It's lovely, it's such a beautiful place and it's a great comfort having him so close. A lot of people think it's silly, but I don't: you have to experience it before you can say. I wouldn't have wanted to have him cremated – my father was cremated six years ago and that was horrible. You see the coffin slide down and then your imagination takes over – the burning. But they are beautiful peaceful places and my father has a plaque on the wall.

I'm not sleeping much; just a few hours a night. I find that if I do take a pill, I wake at about two. It's difficult, because there's so much to cope with with the others. My husband does take his pills, because he's got his work: he needs them to keep his brain working, apart from the fact that he's still got us to look after. He says he can keep Martin just a foot away: but when he's in the office, and it's quiet, tears just stream down his face.

I shall never get over it. He was so nice. He was so nice to me – he never raised his voice or shouted at me. He was so nice with the other two as well; they never fought at all. He would moan like the rest of them when I needed some heavy work done, but that was just being human. You don't realise, you take them for granted. And you work for twenty years, you try to teach them, show them, and you see it all coming out. It's all there. You can see it all like a bud. He was a man, such a fine man. But now he's not here. He was doing well at school, too: he didn't like work, but then boys don't. Not like girls. We didn't go on at him and make his life a misery. We knew he'd come out all right.

I suppose there's a time to be born and a time to die, and it soon comes. You can't say 'I'm not ready; I don't want to go.' There's nothing you can do. With God's help I shall have to accept it: I thought I was bearing it. I went to church and spoke to God, and I became closer to Martin, strangely enough. I hang on to Martin as if I was hanging on to God. I have to hang on. If I don't hang on I will never see him again. But in no way do I blame God for what happened, he didn't make it happen. The suffering has to be part of my life now. It's the wanting, the wanting. It's a terrible want. But then I have two children and the point of my being here is them.

Everything has gone: I only ever wanted three things in my life. I must have been about seven or eight – I was really very small – and I can remember it to this day. I couldn't stop crying the whole evening: I wanted a horse, a happy home, and Martin. Now everything's gone, I know it has, all the future has gone out of it. His future's gone, and our future has gone. It won't come back; they're both combined, they're not separate. We were always so close as a family. How is anyone to know what it's like? I suppose this is how other people feel too, they must do. We've always been so close. I have dreams at night – I never used to dream very much – and I just cry out, 'Martin'. My whole body goes to move towards him, but my mind says, 'He's not there any more.'

He died a month ago. We had him for a week: well, it wasn't him, he'd really gone: we had his body. The day of the accident was such a beautiful day; a bit windy and cold but the sun was shining and the flowers were starting to come out. Everything was so happy. It was Good Friday and he'd been working all morning on the Peugeot, trying to get it going. We hadn't given him an eighteenth birthday present and we'd said we'd see what we could do about the car. He wanted driving lessons and was going to sell the motorbike in September. He said, 'Dad, it doesn't work,' and Sebastian said, 'When we come back from church I'll take you out in it and start it up by rolling it down the hill.'

He went to the service on his bike and we followed in the car. When we came out of church I nearly didn't go up to him, I nearly went straight to the car, because we came out early. He was laughing and said, 'If you're home before me, put the kettle on for a cup of tea,' and he was smiling as he put his arm round me. I said, 'OK'. It was the last time I spoke to him. I went to the car and a few minutes later we joined a queue just before a big bend in the road. My husband said, 'Oh dear, what's happened? There's been an accident. Pray God it isn't Martin.' But it was the way he said it, it wasn't like he usually said things. I said, 'Don't say things like that,' but I thought, 'Oh God, he means it.' We were sitting in the car and saw the man ahead of us get out. He stopped, and we heard him say, 'Martin's had an accident.' I couldn't stop the children, they ran before I could stop them. I ran as well and just managed to reach him. He was just lying there. There was hardly any damage to the car, just the lamp on the driver's side. He was going too fast round the bend: it's a nasty one that tightens up on you. We've driven around there so often and braked to keep the speed limit. We had so much to do that day; we were going sailing and he was happy. He hadn't been home for weeks. He was eighteen and they're immortal when they're eighteen. You only have to forget for one split second: he took the bend and I know what he did because I've done it so often in the car myself. He opened up the throttle, laughing, happy, and took the bend too wide.

He didn't suffer and that's a great comfort. I think he realised what was happening – he leaned over as far as he could to try and hold the bend but he couldn't. You could see the mark in the road where he'd tried to miss the car. He never regained consciousness. They sent for an ambulance and took us with him: they had to give him oxygen in a side room and I was walking up and down. When the doctor came I said, 'I have to know how he is'; being Catholics I needed a priest if he was about to die. He said he was brain damaged because both ears were bleeding and we must move him to the neurological centre. It was about five minutes before the priest arrived and I could hear his breathing – bad, deep, breathing. He called me, he shouted, 'Oh no Mum, oh no,' as if he knew what he'd done in that split second when he hit the car. It was in his memory and he knew after that he wouldn't be anymore. We knew that he wouldn't know a thing after that. He didn't come round at all.

There wasn't a mark on him, just a tiny scratch across the top of his hairline, just two grazed, tiny little dents. They wanted the helmet so they could do research to find out about the impact. We couldn't understand it, we expected it to be bashed in. He must have been going at forty miles an hour.

They said it was very serious and they couldn't operate. That last day we stayed there for hours: and then I felt something like a rock, a huge ice-cold stone which turned over in my stomach. I thought then, 'That's it.' At 3.15 a.m. four doctors came rushing down the corridor and said, 'He's stopped breathing.' I knew he'd gone. They got me a cup of coffee. The priest helped me very much. Then the doctor came and told me he was dead, that there was no brain movement and he'd never come round. There was this terrific bang inside me. He was very good to me. He cried. It must be as difficult for them to tell us as it is for us to hear it. Some of the sisters were so distant; there's fear there, I can see it now, but I couldn't understand it then. I thought, 'Why don't they tell us? Why don't they say something?' And then you feel inside you don't want them to tell you because you can't bear to hear that word. But it's part of their job.

There was one charge nurse there who did everything he could; he changed Martin's pipes and never moved from his bedside. They sit there and check their eyes every ten minutes. I remember Martin moved his arms in jerks: it sounds a hard thing to say, but it was like a chicken with its head cut off. But this man was on duty the night we took Martin in, and he was so good. He couldn't have been more than twenty-seven and he gave me a packet of cigarettes because I hadn't any with me. He was always so pleasant: he said, 'What have they told you?' and I said, 'Just that they can't do anything, we've got to wait.' He said, 'Don't worry, they have to put him on a breathing machine, have you seen one, do you know what it is?' I said I'd seen one on the television and I wasn't frightened and he said, 'It keeps the pulse going and helps to take the strain off the heart,' and I said, 'Oh, yes, I understand.' He said did we realise that there wasn't much they could do and I said, 'Yes, you are doing all you possibly can, but he does seem to be reacting.' They were using injections and checking with lights. Some people might think it rather cruel but at least he was honest: he said it quite sharply; 'There is nothing there, nothing at all. Have you prepared yourself?' I said, 'I don't know, I think so.' Then he walked to the boy in the next bed who was seventeen and as bad as Martin.

My brother-in-law William is an abbot in a monastery in the Midlands. When the accident happened I said to him,

'Can you organise prayers with your monks?' William went to bed about twelve o'clock the night Martin died, but he couldn't sleep. He got up and walked around, not knowing what was the matter. He couldn't rest so he went down to the Lady Chapel. He said it was about 3 a.m. as far as he could tell. He was praying there for a while, and he thought it might help us if he told us what he'd heard. He doesn't know where it came from or whether it was male or female, but he said that everything went very quiet and everything around was clear and bright. He heard this voice which was crystal clear. It said, 'Now is the time of thy tribulation over. Enter into the joy of the Lord.' He knew then that Martin had gone. A few minutes later, at 3.30, he heard the rest of the monks coming back to pray. He was waiting for our phone call – he couldn't understand why we hadn't phoned, now that he knew that Martin had died. He rang my mother who took the call because Sebastian had gone to collect me from the hospital – and my mother said, 'Martin's gone,' and he just couldn't believe it.

He's there in my mind all the time. He's around, he never leaves me. I'm full of him and the instant I wake up in the morning it's always Martin. I see him on motorbikes, on every one. I can see his face through the visor and it's like a knife piercing my heart.

I have to make myself concentrate: I have to concentrate on the driving I have to do. Everything else I do automatically, because my mind is full of him. You cook, you just do it blind, you don't need to look – you don't know where you are, you're in a daze really. I have to put everything in the diary: there's always so much going on, people coming, and the children's friends. I used to have some of the boys from round here when their parents were away: they were all Martin's buddies – he had lots and lots of friends. We've had lots of fun with the family together.

I haven't really needed a doctor: he's a friend of ours anyway and he came to see us after a few days and said if I ever needed anything he'd be there. I feel if I get to that state I'll just give up. I'm smoking more. The thing that helps me most of all is prayer; I pray a lot, I pray and pray. I love the garden – I always have done and it's a great help. I used to say, 'Thank God it's a lovely day.' I didn't need to say any more, I just used to thank Him for what He'd given me and that I'd got a garden.

My husband is the most wonderful support. We can talk together, cry together, share everything. He's not a person to show emotion: now I don't know whether that's a man's trait that they don't cry, or whether it was how he was brought up, but he said, 'You're seeing another side of me you've never seen.' I said, 'I know, but I knew it was there.' It's wonderful, because he is so kind. Some men might feel that it was a weakness and not want to show it.

He started drinking a lot although he's stopped now. Before the accident he always had a whisky, a meal, a whisky, a chat. Then he started having two doubles before supper and he'd drink three or four whiskies and then two or three brandies. What could I say? I couldn't tell him not to do it: I was smoking nearly thirty cigarettes a day and I knew that was his only release, he'd got enough, going to work and thinking about us and whether he'd ever be able to get his mind straight. It's coming back now, but his spark has gone: it'll come back eventually. He said himself during the second week, 'I must stop this because it's doing me no good, or anybody else.' Martin was very like him in that way, strong and clear-thinking; his mind and his brain were the same. He'd read almost every book in this house.

The week he was in hospital I sorted out his room and his things: we went shopping on the Thursday to get things in for Easter. We bought him a new toothbrush. Then the accident happened and I thought to myself, 'Well if God can raise Lazarus from the dead, if he wants to he can give me Martin back.' But I thought, it can't be what I want, it has to be what God wants. You don't bargain with the Lord, you ask him, and you do whatever is best. I thought I'd better get the room ready in case. I wanted to do the sheets, and all the buttons had come off his favourite shirts – they're still not on. His room was all ready and it's still there just as it was; it'll stay like that.

I didn't realise how many friends he had: more friends

than I shall ever have. He always loved that – he talked to people, he didn't mind what rank or station they were, it never bothered him. He used to say to me, 'Oh, Mum, you've never met so-and-so; I know he's got long hair and wears jeans, but he's a super chap, he's really super, you'll like him.' He used to go deeper than the surface.

I've one friend who's been a marvellous help: we asked her to take phone calls from the hospital and arranged for her to phone William at the monastery. I had to ask somebody to do that. Most of our other friends are in the Midlands.

The letters never stop: I've already started to compile them. Photographs are very precious. And we must write about it – that will be the hardest thing, but we must do it. In September when the ground has settled we can put the headstone up. I've already found a prayer – a beautiful one – to have engraved on it: 'Fear not, saith the Lord, for I have redeemed thee and called thee by thy name and thou art mine when you walk through the floods. The water will not cover thee because I shall be with thee. When ye walk through the flames, the flames will not burn thee because I am the Lord thy God.' And there's another one about the virtuous man who died before his time – I haven't decided which one to have yet.

It will be a different life. It won't be the life we wanted. It's a part of you which is gone and you can't get it back. But if you look at it another way, he won't have the agonies that we have. He won't have the sin on his soul that I've got on mine. He didn't live long enough, there wasn't enough harm in him. He'll have gone straight there, I know he's there.

I wrote to him once: I was a bit worried because we used to go to Mass on Sunday mornings and he'd say things like, 'Oh, Mum, do I have to get up?' and I thought I ought to write to him. I wrote a very long letter and said, 'It doesn't really matter whether you believe there's a God, as such, but there is something there that's higher than anybody else in whatever shape or form He is. It's different for everybody but you have to make your own way and you have to believe in your own God and you have to find Him yourself. He's there and He'll never leave you. Never do any harm to anyone, always do the right thing if you can. He will say "You've tried". You must have your own rules for life, because you're nearly a man. If you work out as well as your father I shall be that proud.'

I was so proud of him, and he knew that. He knew he was loved because we'd given him our time and our love: you can't do any more than that, I would have hated it if I'd been one of those mothers who shout at their children and drag them around and then give them a sweet to make up for it. They don't know what they're doing. Although I won't say I've never clouted him: I'm human.

He was so tall, even when he was small. His teachers used to say, 'We have to remember he's only five; we think he's seven.' At three he would have a conversation and we never spoke baby-talk to him. He was so tall and so strong, like my father. He had a mop of hair: they used to call him 'Fuzz' at school. It was very thick, natural hair like Sebastian's. I used to despair sometimes: I wouldn't want to own him with all that hair and his jeans, but just before Christmas he said, 'I must get my hair cut,' and, 'I want a clean shirt.' I said, 'Oh, this is something new!' All the teaching and love were showing: it was all there. He used to call me 'Old dear'.

Most of the time I feel numb, even when I cry. It helps to cry, I think you have to cry. I can be hoovering and suddenly I just cry. I can be in the garden mowing the lawn, or driving along the road, and I have to stop, I just can't see where I'm going. Something happens and I keep thinking to myself, 'I know you're there inside my head' but I have to think of something else! The crying does relieve things, though.

Talking about him doesn't make it worse, because he was so nice. I want to talk about him, a lot. I talk to my husband and I can talk to my friend. She's always there, and she says 'When you want to cry, you cry'. She's had quite a lot to cope with and she understands. But I can't stand crowds of people: everything they say seems so petty. I think, 'If only you knew how lucky you are.' I just can't face them, and that upsets me. I want to cry when I hear them talking about silly useless things that don't matter at all. I used to think I was getting old because I'd lose patience with them.

We try to go on in the same way as before: you have to. We plan to go sailing again this weekend. We do these things. I think we do them more because we've got the other two, and their lives are only just beginning. It's affected Stephanie very much, really very much. In the last year the sort of friendship they developed was very special: they were brother and sister and that was lovely to see. Now it's all gone. You have to carry on for them, you have to. You don't want to: the last thing in the world I want to do is to go sailing. I'm quite happy just to be here, to potter in the garden. I'd rather stay at home. But it can't be because it would be bad for them and bad for me. Philip said a couple of weeks ago when Sebastian wanted to go down and make sure the boat was OK, 'I hope you won't mind, Daddy, I don't want to hurt you but it's not the same when Mummy's not there.' He's such a dear. I thought, 'Oh, dear, this is the last thing in the world I want to do,' but Sebastian said I must make the effort for him.

Our life's finished but theirs isn't, and we must do everything for them. You can't just pick up from where you left off. He was so much a part of us, we had him for so long. But we have to cope, for the sake of the other two. If we didn't have the other two I really don't know what we'd do.

I must try to find a job – I'd like to work with animals; and we must make the effort to go away on holiday. But I can't make plans any more. I don't want to live too long. It's funny how we touch each other's lives in a kind of pattern.

I find I have the radio on all the time; the voices fill the house, but I don't listen to what is said. I don't find television relaxing: Martin's still there, all around me, and I remember the programmes we used to watch together. Funnily enough Sebastian and I were listening to Mozart's fortieth symphony the other night: it helps Sebastian tremendously but it hadn't affected me up until then. At the end I just couldn't stop crying. Everything seemed born again and came to life. The music expresses so well the gaiety and the laughter of Martin. How could a person invent such music? Usually I find it too intense to listen to, and I'm too deep in my own thoughts anyway to concentrate. My husband, who used to be a bookworm, can't read a book now. He was a real pal with Martin. He controls it very well, but it's so awful, it's so hard. I don't think too much of what *could* have been; it hurts too much.

7

ANNABEL:
her stepbrother

Annabel is thirty, is married to Ben, and they live with their two small sons in the country on the edge of a small village. Just over a year ago her eighteen-year-old stepbrother, Robert, was killed in a car crash. It was the latest in a long line of bereavements: Annabel's mother committed suicide when she was five, and her grandfather shot himself when she was fourteen. Other relatives died also, in a family which, as she explains, was never very close-knit. Like many people who have experienced a series of losses, she has a philosophical attitude to death and a stoical approach to life.

When sorrows come, they come not single spies,
But in battalions!

Shakespeare: *Hamlet*

My father won't talk about death; he's one of those men that won't, so it's very difficult for my stepmother. My husband is the same – they won't talk about it so they bottle it all up inside themselves. It's much worse that way. My stepmother loves to talk about Robert and has very little opportunity I think: while I was staying there last week she talked and talked to me. Since they moved house a little while ago things are much better because when they were in the old family home – which was very much Robert's home – I can imagine that everywhere she went she'd see him there: whereas now she's in a different environment she can bid the thoughts when she wants them to come. It's much happier that way.

It has undoubtedly affected her catastrophically: he was eighteen and the apple of her eye. Only six or eight months previously it was very evident that she and my father were likely to split up and I think that forged a bond that made her much closer to Robert than ever before. I think his death was the final blow. But she's lived through something like that before: her fiancé was killed just before she married him and she said to me once that she always had a feeling it could happen to Robert because he just got every ounce out of life: he was almost too big for it. And this was exactly the same – her fiancé was killed in a plane crash and he was a similar character. But then she says all the time, 'Well, how marvellous that he did get all that out of life.' For eighteen years he did far more with what he had than most. OK it was motorbikes or whatever he wanted to do: he was very fortunate in that funds were there to do what he wanted to do, so in those eighteen years he absolutely packed it in. It's rather nice for her to think back and know that she gave him so much. The question of education comes up here: she said, 'Well, if he'd been away at public school I'd have had so much less of him, whereas I had eighteen years of him.'

She doesn't mourn him now so much; she's a Christian Scientist which obviously gives her a lot of strength. My father isn't and that's another bone of contention. I don't think she mourns him because she still has this belief that she can talk to him, that he is somewhere, which is tremendous.

She has had so many bad experiences of people turning the other way: they didn't want to get involved. They don't know what to say, even after fifteen months. She says she's got used to it now but that at first it was very difficult. In a way it was almost a relief to her to begin with but now she says she knows how they feel and yet a gesture would be so welcome. It's just ignorance on people's part – they haven't had that sort of thing happen to them I suppose. If you've had it happen to you, you know what to do.

I went up for Robert's funeral, which was a cremation: I'd never been to one before, which considering all the deaths that have occurred in my family, wasn't maybe the best one to go to. I found it was quite dramatic in a way, when they draw the curtains. He had just got engaged to a girl who was awfully sweet; I saw her last week and she's getting on very well. I think the young mend, but there were tears in her eyes when she was talking to me and we weren't even talking about him. The last time I saw her was at the funeral and she stood next to me at the front. The vicar was awfully good: he made it a very young funeral. I was amazed, there were so many young people – but then Robert had been involved with motorbike scrambling and trials and so on. He'd always helped a lot of lame ducks, he had a lot of friends, so it was a very young occasion. The sun shone, which psychologically always makes me think things are better, but I did find it very dramatic and chilling to see the coffin there and then at the end to see the curtains drawing, and you know it's gone.

His ashes were scattered on a hill where he had broken some kind of record: the farmer said, 'Yes, of course, if that's where you want to scatter the ashes, do it.' I remember Mummy saying that there were snowdrops and daffodils out at the time and she felt quite happy about it, rather happier, I imagine, than thinking of him buried in the ground. With her kind of belief she doesn't need a place, a grave to visit. There's an entry in the book at the crematorium and they went back there this year to the little chapel there. But there's no plaque or anything like that; they didn't want it, because she still believes that he's there, she believes in her living memories.

I just can't help thinking, what a waste. Yet if it was going to happen it happened, it has happened, and he couldn't have lived a cripple, he wouldn't have wanted that. He's just not made that way. There are some people who have fantastic minds and can write and do all those sorts of things: they can cope with it, but he was 100 per cent physical. When everyone else walked, he would run. I think it would have frustrated him beyond belief.

When I first heard what had happened, I was very shocked. I felt very cold. My initial, immediate reaction was that I didn't want to be left alone. I think the shock numbs you. You go through the motions for weeks and I suppose by the time that's worn off you're beginning to accept it. That's the way one's body reacts; it anaesthetises you in a funny way, and helps you to go through the funeral and to go through everyone saying, 'Oh how dreadful,' and all the rest of it. When you come out of that, you're a bit stronger.

My mother – my stepmother – got a lot of letters, which helped her no end. My father drafted a letter (and it's naughty because I'm not in it) but they sent it to everyone who wrote to them and I thought it was a very good idea. They couldn't write personally to everyone and they felt that something like this was the answer:

'I write on behalf of my wife Doreen, daughter Jo, Robert's fiancé Jane, her family and myself in thanks for your kind expression of sympathy on the death of our beloved son.

'Robert's was an active, joyful life, and whenever he found his parents or friends looking sad, his favourite expression was "Come on then, smile". In this time of sadness and loss, we have gained courage and comfort from that quotation, and I repeat it in this letter in the hope that the philosophy of a young man, taken from us in the springtime of his life, might give strength to those who are left to bear such burdens as come their way.

'Sincerley and in gratitude.'

I think the message in it is, that he wouldn't want us to mourn. Let's do what *he* wants.

It has left a gap; although a gap that wouldn't have been there had it not been for seeing him recently on holiday, six months before he died. My relationship with my family has been so strained for years that it's only now I realise I've got a mother in my stepmother and a sister, be it a stepsister; and I think the same would have happened with Robert. They were so much younger than me. I was the big sister and when I left home I was away for twelve years and it's only now that we're knitting together again really. I feel that with him we would have been knitting together now, but if we'd been knitting together before, then the gap would have been worse. The friendship, the relationship, closeness, were beginning.

My mother took an overdose when I was five, then my grandmother who I'd been living with died, then my grandfather shot himself – and amongst all that there were relations dying off like ninepins. Perhaps it sounds hard to say this, but death was just such a part of my life that I grew up with it. If Ben's granny died tomorrow I'd say, 'Well, you know, that's dreadful,' but I wouldn't be torn apart. I don't know what it would take to do that: even if something dreadful happened to Ben (this sounds dreadful) I know I could cope. It wouldn't leave me a shaking valium-ridden wreck. It all goes back to my upbringing. This seems to be the message, that through suffering you become stronger. It's not a question of being tough, it's a question of being strong.

In many ways sudden death, like Robert's, is a very easy death. With a lingering death you're being prepared for it all the time. But I think there are definitely good ways of dying and bad ways of dying.

I do remember a lot of what it was like when Mummy died although it's extraordinary how things get blotted out and you go through life only remembering certain things. When my children got to that sort of age all the memories came flooding back. I started to compare their childhood with my childhood and the fact that my mother didn't get on with my father although she loved him desperately; so she and I spent a lot of time with her parents in the country. I remember her just as a terribly gentle person, just so gentle. On the morning of the day she died I remember her saying to me, 'Be a good girl, granny will look after you,' and I remember that she said, 'I want to sleep now.' That was in the morning and by mid-afternoon I remember saying to my grandparents, 'It's time Mummy woke up,' and I went to try and wake her up and of course I couldn't. I kept shaking her and I remember realising what had happened. It sounds so dramatic but I remember it clearly because she was making that funny noise that they make when they go into a coma. I feel that her parents must have known because why would they have let her sleep so long? Then there was a tremendous sort of rumpus, and I remember the ambulance coming – it had to drive across a field because they couldn't get through the drive. It was February time so it was dark by the time the ambulance got there and my father was rushing around. I don't know the exact details, but I think she lived for a little while, a day or so, and then my grandmother told me one morning that Mummy had died and gone to Jesus. I remember crying and she said, 'Yes, you have a cry,' but then it was over. Life had to go on. It was rather ghastly in a way because I was immediately boarded out into a convent, virtually within days, it seemed like. They felt it was the best thing for me, and it was also my mother's wish that I went to the convent where she was educated. I remember being given a koala bear which I cuddled so much that it was bald within a very short time. But of course nuns are very compassionate and in time I just got over it, children do. I suppose I did miss her later on, in my teens and so on, but by then I'd become such an independent little thing. I'd boarded for quite a long time, and then I became a weekly boarder. My father had house-keepers and what-have-you which I never liked, and then he met my stepmother and married her. It affected me terribly really, because I always felt I was the Cinderella of the family.

This is why this last eighteen months when we've suddenly become so close is wonderful, because really from the age of eight, when they got married, she and I just never got on. Relations used to come and say to me, 'Are you happy, Annabel?' and I used to think, 'What a crazy thing to ask me when I'm obviously not particularly happy.' There'll always be a few happy times but she wasn't my mother and she had her own young family before she was forty, so in a way I was a skivvy. No wonder when I'd finished my education I left home the minute I could.

I missed my mother terribly when I had my own children. The only really tangible thing I have of her is her first cousin whom she was terribly fond of and they were very close. My father won't talk to me about her: I suppose he feels guilty, he must do. But this cousin and I talk about her a lot and when I had the children she said, 'Oh, your Mummy would have been so excited about it.' But she was with me for so little time really – five years is very little time. Yet I remember such softness and such kindness and such an air of tranquillity around me which was then shattered for good.

I didn't know anything about her funeral; she was

cremated, but because we're such a 'push it under the carpet' family I can never ask my father any of this: everything I know is what I've found out on my own. I didn't know she'd taken an overdose until six or seven years ago when I put one and one together and thought, 'Well . . .' For all my life I had been led to believe that she was poorly and died. I remember once writing to an uncle saying why did Mummy die; he wrote back and said, 'I think you ought to ask your father that,' and something stopped me asking him. I was told by my solicitor: he found out for me because he was appalled that I didn't know – so I half expected it. But it was a bit of a shock, I must confess. What did I feel? I just felt so sorry for Mummy, actually, that she couldn't stand up to the situation, but then we're talking about twenty-five, twenty-six years ago. I think nowadays women are stronger, they know also that they can get out of these situations. And I did feel angry with my father. This is obviously why he didn't tell me, because he didn't want me to react against him. In recent years, when he knows I obviously know, he's been quite cautious. He does come out of it in a bad light; he came down last year and said, 'Let me extend your house for you.' He hasn't got the money but he thought that would make up for everything, which is so silly because my feelings towards him have never changed. They've never been that well defined. I said to Mummy the other day, 'I've never leant on either of you, I've had to be independent from the age of five when my mother died and I still am.'

I don't need to lean on anybody: perhaps when you've taken all those knocks you feel it's safer not to. I certainly don't lean on Ben and he wouldn't like me to. When a similar situation arises or if I'm in a muddle I go and cry on somebody else's shoulder. You can't say that your upbringing doesn't affect you, it jolly well does, through and through. Not talking to me about my mother alienated me from my father completely. He must have thought, all through my life as he saw me getting older, 'Well, should I tell her now?' but never has. Had he told me at an early age I would have felt that he was sharing it with me and that he was trusting me. So I really had to go behind his back and find the death certificate and all that sort of thing: at least my solicitor did. Maybe it's cowardly of me, maybe I should have faced my father, but I don't think it's my responsibility: it was his. I wouldn't expect my two children to come to me and ask what had happened if they'd had something like that. It would be up to me to tell them.

Now I get on with my stepmother very well; I feel, as I said, that I have recently discovered I have a mother. The other night when I was staying there I was out with my stepsister and when I got back Mummy was very low and she just cried and cried on my shoulder and I thought, 'It's tremendous really, that she can, and that I can help her.' However, I do feel that it takes a long time to kick away what's gone before. When she came down last September – the first time she had come down ever – I was still sort of Cinderella-y, but I've got over that completely now. I feel we are together now. In fact I heard myself saying, 'Well, come on, if things are that bad you can always come and live here.' Which is something I would never have thought to have heard myself saying in the past. So something good has come out of all this.

I was fourteen when my grandfather shot himself and the most traumatic thing about that was the actual fact that he had done it. I thought that was just dreadful, terrible. He did it because he couldn't live without my grandmother. He was a little Hitler, he was a dreadful man; he was a farmer and I laugh about him really because he was just such a character and I love characters and eccentrics, they appeal to me. He adored me and I spent a lot of time out there with him both before and after my mother died. He always wore hobnail boots and he'd plonk through the village in them. But when my grandmother died of a heart attack he just couldn't cope: she was his second wife, his first wife committed suicide for some reason or other and put her head in the gas oven. It just goes on and on! But no, he just couldn't cope and he was very healthy so he knew that no way through natural causes was he going to be put under the ground. He felt that this would be the only way. He must have loved her; although he was a dreadful tempestuous man and shouted at her all the time. Yet I always remember the night my mother died I slept in the same bed with them, in the middle, and he kissed her and I thought it was so amazing that he showed her affection like that; I thought that was rather sweet. He'd apparently said to all his buddies that he couldn't go on living and therefore he was going to end it all. Again, I suppose I just accepted it – he wrote a letter to say that he wanted to be with his wife: this was about a year after she died.

As I say, it's just one thing after the other: I think he tried to be happy for a long while. Some of the pressure was due to my father who kept taking me over to see my grandfather, which must have been very gruelling for him. It must have been very difficult: my father after all had been responsible for my grandfather's daughter's death. Then he shot himself and that was dreadful and my father had to tell me that – he did tell me this time. Again there was just a kind of numbness. It sounds awful but the dreadful thing about it was that it got on the front of the local paper, because he was a local character, and it said 'He left just one granddaughter, Annabel' and at the age of fourteen that was terrible. I knew that all my friends would see it and I cared terribly about that. Somebody said, 'It'll be a nine day wonder,' and I remember counting the days and saying a week later, 'Well that's seven days and I've only got two more days to go.' I really believed in the nine day wonder and it must have worked.

But again I didn't go to his funeral: I think he was buried – I'm fairly sure he was. I should have gone, at that age I jolly well should have done. Particularly as I was his only relation. He'd said that there were to be no flowers and I remember that I just sent a posy of roses and that was all the flowers he had. It's awful to say it but after the nine day wonder I got over it: I was getting so blooming used to it. Some families are so close that they know exactly what granny's doing that day and what grandpa's doing that day and what so and so is doing that day. But by virtue of my situation it never was like that.

Both my mother and my grandfather are too far back to feel the same way as I do about Robert – that he's there, somehow. I remember them through photographs, and through various small things I did with them. Grandfather always used to take me to the village show – that sort of thing. Whereas Robert is almost tangible, in a way: I suppose it's because I don't want to forget him. He was here for so little time. Eighteen years is such a short stretch – so why not be able to remember him? I encourage my boys to talk about him: they just accept that he's gone to Jesus. For a little while they couldn't believe it – they couldn't believe that someone could be here one day and gone the next. They look at great-granny at ninety-four and say well she might die tomorrow and that's just a child thinking, 'Crikey, at that age you can't go on much longer.' But Robert, to them, was a bundle of energy, so how could that go? I suppose children think of death with illness, or age, they don't think of it as coming out of the blue like that.

8

SALLY:
her mother

Sally and Mark are both thirty-nine and have two little boys, Matthew and Tom, who are five and two. They both work for the broadcasting media and live in a quiet cul-de-sac off a square in north London. Ten years ago Sally's mother died of a heart attack at the age of sixty-six. Her father, who was then sixty-seven, is still alive and has since remarried. Sally was their only child, although they fostered a boy who was a little older than Sally. Although she was twenty-nine when her mother died, and it happened a decade ago, she explains what a fundamental effect losing her mother had on her.

Blow out, you bugles, over the rich dead!
There's none of these so lonely and poor of old,
But, dying, has made us rarer gifts than gold.

Rupert Brooke: *The Dead*

Two years before she died my mother had a hiatus hernia with very bad pain and she'd had an operation for that: I think they discovered then that she had some kind of heart abnormality. She never looked really well after that: she always looked bluish around the lips. I wasn't with her when she died: she lived near Cardiff and until about a month before it happened, we had been living in Bristol which was only forty-five minutes drive away. It was unfortunate in a way: I really wonder how much all the worry of our move to London had to do with it – she always worried so much about what we were doing. We had only been in London about two weeks when she had her first crisis, so of course I was at a distance. I used to travel up and down constantly, and having started a new job which made heavy demands on me, it wasn't easy. She died about a month later: my father phoned me at about eight in the morning and I went down there straight away.

I knew she was dying, because she was such a lively, active sort of person: whatever illnesses she had had were always thrown off in a trice because she was a happy family person. It's awful to say it but I was willing her to die in the end because I couldn't bear to see her lying there like that. I remember holding her hand and saying, 'You mustn't give up, you must try.' And I knew she couldn't; I knew she would have to give up.

Nevertheless, when my father phoned, it was a shock. I knew she had had a severe attack: whether, if she had gone to a different hospital, or if her problem had been diagnosed before, the outcome would have been different, who can say? We felt some rage against the hospital she was in because one of the nurses there was so unpleasant to her and told her how uncooperative she was: she really was horrible to her, and we thought it was appalling. We did get a formal apology, so at least there was that. I was anxious, when we wrote to complain, not to make it seem as if we wanted revenge, but I felt that somebody who could be so horrible to someone who was, as it turned out, mortally ill, really oughtn't to get away with it.

I couldn't actually talk to my mother about dying because we all hoped she wouldn't: but I felt that she knew that it was pretty bad. We were all so dependent on her in various different ways. I used to be able to talk to her a lot: I wouldn't say that I could tell her everything, that would be sentimental of me. But I suppose the basis of my grief afterwards was this feeling of being so intertwined: you can't tell where the one person starts and the other begins. I felt there would never be anyone so completely on my side again; it is what I hope my children will feel about me. The relationship with your mother is absolutely irreplaceable: there is nothing like it or that could be like it. My father is very nice and we do love each other, and we get on now very well; but we are very alike and my mother has always been the peacemaker. Taking that away has had quite a firm effect on our relationship.

He has remarried; in fact, he's been very lucky. It's all turned out wonderfully. He has a cousin who did a crude piece of match-making and it came off: they all went on holiday together and my father and Sylvia fell in love. My father and I had this extraordinary conversation on the Bristol Downs in his car when he said, 'Just think Sally, how would you feel if I got married again? Just think about it: it's nothing definite, you know.' And I found them asking me if they could get married. It was strange, them asking for my permission. I had no negative feelings at all about it whereas my mother's sister and my foster brother both did. The day they got married we just had a few drinks at their house and my foster brother took me on one side and said, 'I can't see that this is right, can you?' and I had to say, 'Well, yes, I haven't got any doubts.' I obviously felt sad that it had been necessary for him to find another person, but when I think of how he was when Mummy died: he lost weight, he got skinny, his clothes were hanging off him, he was skin and bones. He was very noble, however: when people said, 'Oh, you must come around,' he took them at their word. He joined a bowls club and found himself a new circle of friends. He learned how to cook and crew a boat because he was determined not to depend on me. Considering he had been pampered all his life, it was very good of him.

So he deserved to have someone nice. He was saying even a year afterwards, 'There doesn't seem any point in going on living.' I thought that was just awful: they had been so close since the day they married, and that was for thirty years. But this wasn't, 'Please marry me for companionship's sake,' it was a real romance. She had been on her own for fifteen years and she had to be courted. It's worked out very well. I think men adapt less well than women do to living alone. But she was so delicate about it: she always expected me to feel ambivalent about her and it took her a long time to realise that I wasn't at all. She would be afraid to wash up in her own home – my old home – when I was there, because she was aware that she was taking my mother's place. My father was a bit naughty really, it would have been much better if he had sold the house and moved somewhere else; but they wanted a bungalow and there aren't many in that area. He sold their furniture though, his and my mother's, and got a new bed: and they moved from the room where they always slept into another room. Sylvia is very good at managing and she is just a super person. It's lovely that there is a happy ending.

She hasn't replaced my mother, but to some extent there is a granny figure for the children, and a mother-type figure for me. One funny thing is that Matthew has a little bit of a thing about death. I had never told him what had happened – I thought I'd wait for him to ask about his granny; so Sylvia was always referred to as Nan since that was the name she wanted to be called by the children. Somehow he picked up that she wasn't my mother, and he asked, 'Where is your Mummy?' I told him she was dead. He seemed to take it in his stride, but unfortunately when he was nearly four a little friend of his had told him that she didn't have a Daddy and he came home to me and said, 'Mary said that her Daddy is dead,' and from then on we had a series of questions: 'Will you die, will I die?' and he was so concerned about it. He was obsessed, and very upset. He deduced from watching television that dying meant pain: 'If I die, I want to die in hospital.' And, 'When will I die?' He unfortunately stumbled on the fact of our mortality about two years before he was effectively able to cope with it, and he kept asking questions about it all the time. Naturally we weren't going to tell him that we won't die because you can't tell a child lies like that. I am a Quaker, and Mark is a member of the United Reformed Church, but I don't have the same kind of belief in an afterlife as he does, so Mark was able to be more helpful to Matthew than I was.

I didn't find my own religious beliefs very much help in the loss of my mother: I still feel that her presence is somewhere, and I think of her every day in some way or other; she just goes through my mind. I often dream of her and I dream that she is still alive. There are so many things that one regrets in life, and the whole thing about grieving is that there is always some guilt in it, to some extent: I regret two things. One, that I was so adamant that I would never have any children; I think that was partly saying, 'I'll never be like you, I'll never lead your kind of life,' and partly for the very good reason that I was far too immature in those days. But I wish she was still alive to see her grandchildren, and for them to know her, because she was such a super person. My rubbing it in that I would never have children was very adolescent. The other regret is that she didn't live to see how interested I have become in so many of the things that she adored, like sewing and all kinds of craft work: part of the reason that they are, as subjects, very much part of my work now is that they are something to do with her: it's a sort of unfinished business. I found a quotation the other day: 'Like so many gifts from parents to children, these gifts from his father to him were very slow in maturing.' It is very true for me: I watched my mother sew and she sewed very well: she made all my clothes for me as a child and some also for me as an adult, which I can't bear to throw away now. She always wanted me to have a good academic education and was thrilled when I got a good degree and a good job, but it was only after she died that I realised I could sew as well. Then I felt a sense of mission to make those crafts respectable: she, like many others, never rated the things she did superbly. I'm vindicating my mother to a degree, and I think of her when I am planning my work.

I did feel guilt when she died. I felt I had been a very inadequate daughter and that I had often hurt her; that I failed to live up to her expectations of me, not in worldly terms but in what she expected of me as a daughter, which was to love her. I felt I hadn't; I still don't know if I made it clear to her that I did love her. I think I was probably a very difficult person. On the other hand, during her last illness I went down and sat with her: I took a fortnight off work and took all the trouble to cook her her special diet food. As well as being nasty to her from time to time, I did see her a lot then and take her little presents. But I could never be in every way what she wanted. She was far too interested in me, and that is one of the reasons why I now work: I felt she was too bound up in me, living her life through me too much, and I resented that.

I didn't see her after she died; I didn't want to. She was buried in the local cemetery and all the family came to the funeral. I wish she had been cremated rather than buried: I hate to think of her being down there. But I promised her that she would be buried as she hated the idea of being burned. I can hardly bear to visit the grave: I force myself to go perhaps once every two years. I have tried to tell my father that he mustn't be upset that I don't go, but it's difficult. I did see her actually being buried: I remember people saying, 'Oh, no, don't go,' but I'm glad I did. It makes it more real in a way, and I'm glad there was a funeral: I think all those rituals are very helpful. I cried solidly throughout the service: I don't think I have ever cried so much in all my life. I had wonderful support from my family: later on, my father and I would cry together.

I think the most awful moment was when her possessions were returned from the hospital. It was terrible: I just cried and cried. She was buried with her wedding ring on so we didn't have to worry about that: it's so pathetic. I stayed with my father for about a fortnight and then he came to stay with us for about a month. He was very good and controlled, but he looked grey. I'd wake up and churn: Mark was wonderful, he understood that I had to cry, and he let me. I was determined that my father and I would talk about her, and we did, almost incessantly, for quite a long time. About her, our memories, and the way she died. I think that's something you need to go over and over. We were lucky at that time because a very close friend of my mother's from nearby came in day after day and just let us talk at her, which was amazing. She was such a nice person and I thought it was absolutely incredible. I dimly appreciated how super it was of her at the time, but it taught me a lot: it taught me that you mustn't keep away from people who are bereaved, you must offer your help and just go around and be there and let them cry or talk or whatever.

It was an extraordinary period: I found that I was un-naturally calm or else totally hysterical: I was numb-calm. I was able to organise the funeral, and I remember going out and buying writing paper and stamps and envelopes and sitting down at the table and writing about twenty letters. It amazes me, looking back on it, how I could have been so cool. Yet it was helpful having something to do, not to be sitting around with this awful gap that's been left. I remember thinking, 'I must have a hat for the funeral.' I never wear hats and I knew I'd throw it away afterwards, but I took the whole morning choosing it. Strange. That awful pain, that feeling in my stomach, lasted for several months. I went back to work and just flung myself into the new job. I was very unsure that I could cope with it, and of course I had my grief to cope with at the same time. I was manic in terms of energy: I had the energy to do anything. I went into an orgy of travel and work: I just didn't want to think. It was a nervous restless-ness, and looking back on it, I recognise now that I was very, very depressed. I was in and out of the doctor's surgery all the time with complaints of one kind or another. I had backache: my mother had had backache and I was terrified that I had inherited hers. I became a complete hypochon-driac, that's the form my depression took. I had lots of trivial infections, I wasn't eating properly, I didn't sleep very well although I've never been a heavy sleeper. I connect that time with a constant feeling of anxiety, of panic, with no rational basis at all. I cried a lot, but I suppose the worst thing about it was the feeling of aimless dreads, of no hope; that everything was going to turn out bad. It was a dreadful sort of pessimism.

I have become her in some ways. I do very much feel her still as a force in my life. I feel muddled about what I feel in religious terms: her death didn't give me an assurance of the afterlife: I felt the finality of it. At first I couldn't accept that she was actually dead, I couldn't believe it, and I would wake up and think, 'It can't be true, it can't have happened, no it hasn't.' The real living person is still there: all her possessions are around and you can't believe it is so final. My mother's old friend and her sister got rid of the clothes: I don't know who else could have done that. There is no point in a wardrobe full of clothes that somebody else has worn, but there is something so awful about clearing out everything that belonged to someone. Sentimental though it may be, that's why I hang on to those few bits that she made for me, and I'll never get rid of them. I've got a piece of embroidery that she started and never finished, and I'll never part with that. I have got a photograph of her as a young woman, but the thing is that I look very like her: when I look at myself in the mirror I can see her, and that's disconcerting; I think it must be to my father, too, because I resemble her so much.

Gradually, with time, I came to terms with her death when I realised that I had begun to cry for myself and not for her. It was becoming an indulgence. Mark never said a word to me, he let me cry it out, but it was self-pity in the end: I don't know what the difference is between self-pity and genuine grief, but six months after she died I began to realise that if I was still crying, I was crying for me and not for her. What has helped me to come to terms with it is partly that I now realise that she did give me something so tremendous, and that although she is dead, what she gave me lives on. I look like her, I am interested in the things that she was interested in, and the most important thing of all is that the whole way I approach my children is totally conditioned by her. The fact that she loved me so intensely, and I drew back from her love, I know must have hurt her; nevertheless I had a very secure, happy, loving childhood and that is an inestimable gift for a parent to pass on to her child, because it means that you are more likely than not able to do the same for your own children. When I say things to my two, although my memories don't go back in detail that far, I feel she must have said those things to me. Those things you absorb from a parent: and you can get the reverse, like violence and hate. But I think I learned from her how to be a parent, and there is nothing better than that. I wished she had lived long enough to see that I had learned that lesson, that I had become a more mature person, mature enough to have children myself. Her death did make me grow up in a funny way. It made me realise that we are all on our own.

I feel guilty that, as an able-bodied teenage girl, I allowed myself to be waited on by her when my mother was doing a full-time job. She was the one who did the double shift: she was keeping this household of five able-bodied people, and I think it was one of the reasons that I didn't have children right away, that I didn't fancy that role as I observed it. But she, like me, needed to work: she had so much energy, and the reason I want to work is that I saw her do it. Partly she saw it as an escape from home, although she took her house-work very seriously: but her heart was never in that alone. She was a very good friend to several people, and in her untrained way was a social worker as well as a good mother and housewife and it's no wonder she had a heart attack and died, prematurely really: if there is such a thing as premature death. One's expectation is threescore years and ten, but should it be? I used to look at the very old lady living next door to us and think, 'What right have you to be alive when my mother is dead?' I felt a kind of anger at her for having died: why couldn't she still be alive? Why couldn't she have got all of us to do more in the house? Except that, as she saw it, it was her duty and privilege to do things for us.

I found myself very isolated by people and they didn't know what to say: there was one couple in particular who we had helped in their troubles, and the husband never said anything to me, not even that he was sorry to hear that my mother had died. I wanted to talk about it but I felt that I couldn't, because I knew I would cry and that would em-barrass him. It had quite an effect on our friendship: I didn't want to see them because I couldn't be myself. His father had died the year before and I'd said to him, 'I'm awfully sorry,' and he'd just brushed it aside. That was the last of the friend-ship. People at work were wonderful though; one in parti-cular, who in spite of no experience of close bereavement himself, had the imagination to know how I was feeling, and he was super to me.

In a sense death is always unexpected: and yet should it be? It's so much a part of everyday life. Our expectations are so ludicrous: we secretly believe that we are immortal, so we don't talk about death. We are not very good at dealing with death, but we are expert at shoving it under the carpet.

9

PENNY:
her mother

Penny and Paul live on Paul's farm in East Anglia: she is thirty-one and before her marriage she worked with handicapped children. Paul, thirty-five, is a farmer. When Penny was five and a half her mother died of cancer of the liver at the age of thirty-eight. Penny has an elder sister Christine, and a brother Mark, who is two years older than herself. She subsequently acquired two stepsisters when her father remarried four years after the death of her mother. She herself has now got two little boys of her own, Robert who is three and Toby who is one and a half.

Death is the veil which those who live call life:
They sleep and it is lifted.

Shelley: *Prometheus Unbound*

I was five and a half when my mother died. I didn't actually have any reaction at all to her dying; in fact I can remember very well my father telling me the news. We were staying with some friends and he came over to see us one Sunday afternoon. My sister had already been told and she was in the drawing room with him, in tears. She was thirteen and had been very close to my mother because there had been six years during the war when she had never been separated from her; she wasn't very close to my father because he had been away. My brother was also very close to my mother, but nobody realised it at the time: he was seven when she died. We were told that our father had come to see us, and we

91

went down to the drawing room. Christine was sitting there in tears and Daddy just said, 'Your mother has died.' My brother said, 'Oh, no, Daddy,' and sat down and looked very quiet. I said, 'Oh, yes,' almost casually; I can remember saying, 'Oh, yes, can we go for a walk now?' That was my only reaction at the time, which must have been awful for him, I think; or maybe it was easier, I don't know. I have always thought that perhaps it was a little hurtful to him that I didn't react at all.

It didn't really seem as though it was an experience that was very close to me, because my aunt had been looking after us for several months. My mother was taken into hospital in the August and when she was sent home we had to leave because she couldn't stand the noise. So we were sent off in September to stay with some local friends who had children of a similar age, in the care of my aunt, to whom I got very close during that time anyway. I just thought we were having a holiday, although I don't think that Christine felt that way at all. We saw my mother for a very short time every Sunday.

She had cancer just about everywhere: she died of cancer of the liver ultimately: it was the liver that finally made them take her into hospital. I didn't discover that until I was sixteen: my father would never tell me. He just said that she died of liver trouble and that was all I knew. It was so silly of him not to tell us: I felt that we should have known. Any doctor that ever sees you about anything remotely important wants to know your family history and it's quite indicative of some things if your mother has died of cancer of the liver.

At the time, I didn't feel any loss at all; not until my father married again when I was nine. Up until then I had been very close to my old nanny and all my emotions were involved with her. She stayed on until my father married again and then we didn't have a nanny any more. So in fact Nanny had been my mother-figure for those four years. My father tells me now that she was the most extraordinary old biddy and I'm sure she was. I can remember what she looked like but I can't remember anything about her: I just happened to latch on to her, and she was obviously very fond of me: I was very fond of her and it was a vital relationship at the time. In a sense she was my mother for four years. I went to boarding school the summer term just before my father married again and when I went to school I missed Nanny: she was the person I missed. And she left; because with my father re-marrying there was no point in her being there. I missed Nanny dreadfully, terribly.

I can remember that when I got to puberty I really missed not having a mother, because Jean, my stepmother, has never taken the place of a mother in that sense. I have never felt an emotional bond with her, and I never will. When a girl reaches puberty, she does definitely need a mother; some-body who has been through it all and to whom she can relate very closely, and I didn't really have that. I missed her even more desperately after Robert was born: that was when I really needed a mother. I got very low after a few months and was very depressed, and it was my mother-in-law who was most useful to me at that time. She never questioned, she knew that I was depressed and that I missed my mother. She was very quick to latch on to that and she said, 'You know, I'm to take the place of your mother now that you're married to my son.' That was very generous of her: at the time I didn't fully appreciate it but now I do.

But I definitely, definitely needed a mother at that time and I did need the mother I had lost. I think she was very like me although I don't remember her well enough to be sure. I can remember her looks, I can remember certain moments in the life we shared that were very special and I think that she was a very special person: I have heard from a lot of people that she was very special. I don't think I am half the person she was, but in some ways we are similar. She was an understanding sort of person and we both care about what other people feel and what other people think, and we don't write off suffering. I'm sure she would never have written off any form of mental or emotional illness as, 'Oh, dear, the poor child is going batty for a bit': she would have been absolutely with me all the way. I'm just imagining what she would have been like, but I feel that this is the sort of person that she was.

The fact that she couldn't see Robert as a grandmother was very painful: I missed her for that, desperately. I really wanted her there. I'm sure that your mother is the most important person next to your husband after your first baby is born. It's all part of the system going on, it's a part of them. And they can give you so much reassurance too, because they've been through it and to you it's all unknown. My sister was marvellous when it came to that; she came and stayed for a few days when I came out of hospital. But it would have been nice to show him off to my real mother, definitely. Christine was never really a mother-substitute even though she was so much older than myself. She was always a very good person to talk to though because she had very much the same feelings as myself. She missed my mother most dreadfully: my mother left her in puberty and she had some very strange, weird reactions to the whole thing. She ran away from school as a protest at my father marrying my stepmother, not because she didn't like school – she loved school – but because she decided it was a good way of getting through to somebody that she didn't really like what was going on at home.

The teenage years came and went; when you feel down or blue as you do when you're a teenager, you need a certain amount of sympathy as well as a certain amount, probably, of being told to pull yourself together and to stop being so morbid. Every time I did feel a little lonely in the world, and not quite certain which way to go, I always thought about my mother. That was invariably the time when I always thought about her and I could have done with having her there.

Another problem when I was a teenager was that I had the most appalling acne. Rather than anybody doing anything about it, it was ignored: I was told not to put on too much make-up because that would make it worse, but nothing was ever done about it medically. I decided when I was about seventeen that something really must be done so when I left school I persuaded my stepmother to take me to see a skin specialist, who cured it in no time. So I had to suffer all those years, and I'm sure if I had a child with that condition, which is jolly distressing for a teenager, I would do everything I possibly could. I always thought, 'My mother would never have let me get into this state.'

Another time when I definitely missed her was when we started to worry that something was wrong with Toby, when we noticed that he was not developing normally. We went through weeks and weeks of not knowing what was wrong, or if anything was wrong, and then he was ill and taken into hospital. Nobody was in the least bit interested: he was only in for three nights each time, but nobody, my mother-in-law or my stepmother, suggested coming to see Toby in hospital. I thought that was pretty astonishing: if my daughter had had a child in hospital I'd be there doing something practical; or at least holding her hand at the bedside. I was sitting by him for three days and could have done with a little more support at the time. Of course I think that my mother would have been there. I'm sure she would. It was a very worrying time: she would have been able to tell me what we were like as children. My father has forgotten – fathers don't on the whole remember unless there is something outstanding that the child either does or does not do. But my mother would have been able to throw some light on the problem: she probably would have said, 'Well, Christine didn't do that either, and Mark didn't do this, and you didn't do such and such so he just has a combination of all of you.' But she wasn't there to tell me; it would have been a great help, I think, still.

She was buried in the churchyard where we were living in Derbyshire. The churchyard bordered on to our field and she was buried with the gravestone actually backing on to the wall. She loved the house – my parents built it themselves – and she loved the garden and everything about it. The grave is looked after: my father pays somebody a small amount every year just to keep it in good condition and if any of us go back to Derbyshire, we always go to see it. I took Paul to see it the summer after we got married and he was moved to tears by it. He had never seen a grave of anyone so young who would obviously have played such an important part in his life, had she lived. The whole thing moved him very much. I was quite surprised because he had never known her. I didn't think it would, but he said that it absolutely choked him: he was completely silent for about half an hour, which I thought was very touching. I really appreciated it.

In my teens, if ever I went down to the village I always walked that way, because there was a public footpath going straight past the grave. I always used to stop and I did find it comforting. I used to take people to see it: I think now perhaps that was a strange thing to do. If I took friends home from school for a weekend, I always used to take them to see my mother's grave. Looking back on it, and putting myself in their position, I think it must have been very awkward for them but that never occurred to me. I just thought it was something that was rather special: my mother's grave, something that everyone ought to see. I think it probably embarrassed them terribly: I think it would have embarrassed me at that age. But I used to do it from the age of about ten onwards.

Funnily enough, her death didn't make me closer to my father. I have never been able to talk to my father until just recently, although I still don't feel I'm very close. I find him a very difficult person to talk to: he is terribly shy, terribly reserved, and he has never discussed the vices of life, if you like, with me. I think they are all things you should discuss. However, we recently had a very long discussion on some topic and his point of view definitely changed: he suddenly realised that you can talk about these things and you can't just dismiss them. I suppose I can say that my relationship with him is closer: I can talk to him better than I could, at any rate.

Losing my mother, for me, wasn't a crippling loss certainly. There have been compensations all the way along. I have made very close friends always, maybe much closer because I have needed friends just that bit more. I don't think I would be any different if I hadn't been through it myself, and I don't think I'm necessarily a stronger person as a result. Maybe I'm lucky in that I was a person who could cope with it. But I wouldn't say that the loss of my mother at a very vulnerable stage in my life has made me a different person: it has made me just that bit more sympathetic towards other people, possibly.

I did feel envious of people who still had their mummies though. I've always thought that it would be rather nice to have two parents that you could call Mummy and Daddy. I always longed to have someone I could call Mummy. It's a dreadful thing in a way, but it was always as if I felt slightly proud of the fact that I had lost a parent and survived it perfectly well. If anyone was to talk about adopted children, or say, 'Isn't it awful that so-and-so has lost their mother?', I would always find a way of introducing the fact that I had lost my mother and I was terribly pleased to be able to explain how she died. I wanted them to know. There was a certain amount of pride in it; it sounds dreadful, I know, but I don't think I was trying to say, 'Look, aren't I marvellous, I've got through it': it was more a need to talk about it.

I was considered too young to go to her funeral. None of us went. Christine didn't go, and I think she should have done. My father totally disagreed with the idea and said that she mustn't. I have always had a horror of seeing somebody dead and maybe that has something to do with it. I never have: maybe if I had seen my mother dead it might not be that way. I don't know. At five and a half it might not have had a very positive effect at all, it might have been a very bad thing. I saw her last on Christmas Day; she died early in January. She was putting on a very brave face and actually got out of bed for a while: it's very common with cancer patients to rally a week or two before the end comes. I didn't know that she was dying, so I wouldn't have known to have said goodbye to her. I don't know if my mother in her way said goodbye to me: I can't remember. Apparently she didn't know she was dying but I think anyone who's dying must know that they are: they may not ever let on, but I'm certain they do.

Christine found it a crippling loss: it was absolutely desperate for her. She was thirteen and she couldn't stand my father at that stage. When he came back from the war she thought it was the worst thing that had ever happened because suddenly some discipline was introduced into the house. Understandably a child that is looked after by its mother and a nanny for six years is going to be indulged a fair amount when there is so much loss in the world; I think it is understandable to make it up to your child in every way possible. But my father arrived back from the war and things changed, and that started them off on a bad footing; then my brother was born, which didn't help, and then I arrived. I'm sure all these things contributed to making life pretty unbearable for her. In the end she gradually became closer. She has flourished by being married. Before she was married, after leaving school, she didn't know which way she was going; she had no opinions of her own, she had no ideas. She's very practical – she is like my mother in that sense, but all her ideas were put there by someone else and always have been. That may have been made worse by the fact that my mother wasn't there encouraging her to use her own initiative. When she got married she suddenly realised that she was an individual in her own right, had her own family to bring up, and a husband who is a very shy person and needs her support. That has strengthened her no end. I would say she's gone from strength to strength in the last fifteen years.

She had a hellish puberty and if you asked her she would say that she did need her mother then, as well as at certain times since she has been married, having her children for example. She was very hurt when her first child was born in Iraq: neither my father nor my stepmother went out there to visit them, whereas my mother would have just got on the next plane and gone; I went out to see her but that was a year after the baby was born.

I definitely do have a feeling that my mother is somewhere, in some sense. My sister and I both went to the same school as my mother had been to, and she was very highly regarded by that school, which was extremely religious. Religion was very important and my mother carried it through to later life; it played a very important part in her life. If one believes in God at all, then she has gone to better things. She was a very good person if I can believe what I hear. I include her in my prayers when I remember to say them: I have to say that because I don't say them every night like I used to. She is very important in my prayers and I include her as if she was still there. I'm sure she is still there: she just isn't around in a physical sense, that's all. It does help if you believe in God and things are getting you down; prayer does help. You can say anything to God, things you can't say to other people, and you can make a complete fool of yourself if you like. He sees straight through you so there's no point in pretending. I think my mother probably does too: I'm sure she's taking an active part in whatever is going on here. It's a very positive way of thinking about it: if I feel she knows what I'm doing, then it makes it worthwhile doing things well. She must definitely be being rewarded: nobody who contributed so much to life leaves it at such a young age. He must have a very good reason, I'm sure of that; she had to go on to something better.

I'm certain that if my mother had died now, the religious aspect would have come into it very much sooner than it did. At the age of five and a half, stories about Jesus Christ and early Bible stories are all you've ever heard, and certainly religion as such doesn't come into it. My father never said, 'Mummy's gone to Jesus,' he never discussed it even. He never spoke about my mother's death. When I was sixteen I just had to know what she had died of; I thought, 'This is ridiculous.' My father said, 'I've told you, she had liver trouble.' I said, 'You don't just have liver trouble and die: what liver trouble?' 'She had cancer but we don't talk about it.' I didn't question it at the time but if the subject ever came up again I would say, 'Why don't we talk about it?'

There was one thing that hurt terribly and it has only just occurred to me: when Jean married my father, the house was just as my mother had done it. Her taste and Jean's were totally different and so a new broom swept through the house in no time at all. All the photographs of my mother disappeared, every one. My father hasn't got a single photograph of my mother in the house. He has some in an album but there's not one on display. He didn't put up a protest: perhaps in a sense it was more important to us as children than it was to him because he was starting afresh. He had started a new life in the way that he wanted. But it was awful for us as children to have to accept such a change of atmosphere in our home: she sold all the furniture so not a trace of our childhood home was left.

I was an incredibly independent person until I got married. Then for the first time for very many years I had something definite to lean on, something that I loved to lean on. And I leant, very, very heavily. And I do lean very, very heavily. It's a new experience, it's lovely. It's four years old now but it's still a new experience. Possibly it was slightly alien to me to be so independent before that – probably it wasn't really in my make up. Circumstances had forced it, it was a means of survival. In a way I rather regret that I'm not still as independent as that now. I feel that if anything were to happen to Paul I'd be desperate: but having been able to stand on my own two feet very successfully before, I must surely be able to do it again if I ever had to. I must have the resources, even if I don't feel they're very active at the moment. I've had the practice, if you like. But there we are: all three of us children are very adaptable people; that was the way we were born and that's the way we'll always be.

10

CAROL:
her father

Carol is forty-one. Nearly three years ago her husband left her, completely unexpectedly, for another woman: she was left with their two children, James who is now seven, and Henrietta who is four. Carol comes from a close-knit family; she often visited her parents, and has a brother slightly older than herself and a sister who is a few years younger. About a year ago her father was diagnosed as having cancer, and he died a few weeks later. He was seventy-six, a fit and handsome man who didn't look his age. He had been married to Carol's mother, who was ten years younger than himself, for forty-seven years. Happily he was able to die at home surrounded by his loving family.

Death be not proud, though some have called thee
Mighty and dreadfull, for, thou art not soe,
For, those, whom thou think'st, thou dost overthrow,
Die not, poore death, nor yet canst thou kill mee.
From rest and sleepe, which but thy pictures bee,
Much pleasure, then from thee, much more must flow,
And soonest our best men with thee doe goe,
Rest of their bones, and soules deliverie.
Thou art slave to Fate, Chance, Kings and desperate
men,
And dost with poyson, warre, and sicknesse dwell,
And poppie, or charmes can make us sleepe as well,
And better than thy stroake; why swell'st thou then?

One short sleepe past, wee wake eternally,
And death shall bee no more; death, thou shalt die.

John Donne: *Divine Poems,* X

I had a very close friend who died ten years ago, and I felt awful because I didn't do what I should have done for him before he died: I never said to him the very personal things that I wanted to, that I wouldn't have said in other circumstances. I always regretted that it was too late to say them after he died. Had I not had that previous experience, then I might have regretted things about my father, and maybe I would have felt guilty. I remember saying to my father at that time that I loved him, and that I would never feel the same about life after he died. I wanted my father to know that I loved him there and then: I told him that I had wanted to say things to this other friend that I hadn't found myself able to and that I felt guilty that I hadn't. In a way that experience was a preparation for my father's death, which of course was very much worse; but I knew partly what to expect, which did help.

I knew that my father was dying; it was just about this time last year that he had an operation on his bowel which was successful: what they didn't tell me was that he had secondaries on the liver, because I was going on holiday and they didn't want to spoil it for me. I went to see my father before I went away, and I took one look at him and I knew: I have seen people with cancer before – I had a neighbour who died of cancer of the liver and I had watched her die. That was awful because it took three months and I thought I was going to have to watch my father do the same thing; but for him it was very quick, it was six weeks and he was in bed for the last three. He knew he was dying, we all knew.

There was a very good organisation called the Dorothy House Foundation: it is a hospice which cares for the dying in their homes if they are able to die at home, and they are based in Bath. They handle the psychological as well as the physical aspects of dying. There was no dissembling, we all knew and nobody had to put up a pretence. One very distressing aspect to me was that my mother felt that my husband's treatment of me in some way triggered off my father's cancer; it's possible, but nobody ever knows. I think he did worry about me although he didn't verbalise his feelings very much. He was a very shy person.

I didn't cry at that stage, while he was dying. I cried that first time that I walked in and realised that he had cancer: I remember saying, 'Oh, Father, I love you.' And he said, 'Well, I haven't gone yet, dear.' So he knew, then. I don't think he needed to talk about dying; he was quite ready to die. He was a very intelligent, literary person and had been teaching until two years before he died. He dreaded being an old man: he had taken me to see his brother who had Parkinson's disease and said, 'I hope I don't end up like that.' He was not the sort of man to be an old man; he was quite happy, he knew that his family loved him and he was quite serene.

He died at home. I wrote him a letter, the only really genuine love letter I have ever written, telling him how I felt. I loved my father very much, and my mother read it to him because he was too weak by then to hold a letter. He had lots of letters from old pupils who knew that he was dying, and who told him what they felt about him. In a way he had his obituary notices before he died; he heard all the nice things said about him that most people never get to hear. He had lots of tributes before he died, and that was a very nice aspect of it. The village was very involved – people did everything they could to help. The people from the hospice came out about three times a week and provided sheets and prescribed excellent drugs: he had no pain at all.

Then the week came that he died: I was at home with the children, and my mother phoned and said, 'I think you should come.' Father had called all the family round the bedside to say goodbye: this was on the Wednesday, and he just said goodbye quite serenely and happily. On Thursday he wasn't conscious, and on Friday morning he woke up and said, 'Carol's coming today.' I had made arrangements for the children and was driving down. He never woke up again: by the time I got there I was absolutely desperate because I wanted to speak to him once more. I remember the time the previous week when I had had to get back to the children, when I stood in the door and waved goodbye to him, and he waved to me. I remember his face very well: he smiled, and that was the last time I ever saw him with his eyes open. That Friday when I got there, the doctor shouted in his ear, 'Carol's here,' and his eyelids flickered. The doctor said that when people are dying, hearing is the very last thing to go: all the other faculties go first and they can still hear when they can't answer or move. He had really given up; he had said goodbye to his family, and had decided on his time to go, which apparently a lot of people do. He was so weak: he looked like a sort of Belsen figure, and I was very distressed because he wouldn't wake up. I just wanted him to look at me and to speak to me, but he died between two and three in the morning.

I saw him the next morning: I had always dreaded seeing somebody dead, but I didn't actually mind it at all. He didn't look very different; he looked rather grey, and they had taken his teeth out. He was very thin, just like a skeleton, and he looked ill but he didn't look horrible. Somehow I think we managed a beautiful way for him to die, and he wouldn't have been able to die like that if he hadn't known he was dying. Several people said that they thought so, and the doctor said, 'He had a very good death, if you can put it like that.' He did look almost exactly the same when he was dead. I didn't feel frightened at all: I kissed his forehead and so did my sister. He was very cold.

I did have one or two nasty dreams afterwards, but they have stopped now. For months afterwards, if I couldn't sleep at night, I would see him; not as he was when he was dead, but the evening before when he was dying. It was the most distressing thing because the doctor came to give him an injection and we pulled back the sheets: he was so thin, he was like a skeleton, and he was so tall that his feet hung over the edge of the bed. I said to the doctor, 'You can't leave him like this,' and the doctor said, 'It doesn't matter': he obviously knew what was going to happen. That for me was the worst moment, and it was the moment I relived when I was upset.

In the morning the house was very, very peaceful. I often

wondered what it would be like with a dead person in the house, and I thought it would be awful. I had often thought I would never want to live in a house where someone had died, but it wasn't like that at all, it was very peaceful. My mother was terribly relieved: she has taken it very well, although she has her bad moments. She is extremely religious, which helps her. The woman from the hospice came in the morning – they do a follow-up when the person has died, and she came to see my mother several times afterwards as well. She went with my mother out into the garden, and my sister and I sat downstairs. There was a slightly macabre moment when they came in and took him out on a little sort of camp bed: I didn't like that very much, that was a nasty moment.

Then there was the funeral itself: when I first got to the church it was a beautiful, sunny day; the church was full of flowers and all the village was there, plus a lot of my father's old pupils and friends. There was a big bunch of white and red chrysanthemums from the family on the coffin. I had taken my little boy, who was then six, and all the other children were there, which the person from the hospice recommended. I had wanted it anyway: my mother was against it at first but then came round to it and was thankful. They were absolutely wonderful at the funeral; they were very good in the church, and afterwards one just felt that life went on. I think children should be included on these occasions; they know what is happening, and it isn't beastly. Crematoriums can be a bit grim, but not the church funeral. He was cremated: that was his wish, and I was against it although I have changed my mind a bit since then. My brother and sister and the parson went to the crematorium, and nobody else – the village parson was a friend and that was a help too: we had a lovely address from him. Once the funeral started I – enjoyed it is the wrong word, but it was a happy occasion. People in the church didn't look distressed although they loved my father; and indeed I would have liked another ten years of him, but you can't ask for everything, and I don't think he wanted it.

His ashes are buried in a little Norman churchyard; I had a little stone made and every year I shall put bulbs there. My brother was keen on the idea but my sister didn't want to know anything about it. I was a bit upset but I haven't discussed it with her, my mother wouldn't like to feel that my sister and I were arguing about it. Now that my father's ashes are there, I feel I like the idea better than the mouldering remains. We had a little service there just with my brother and the parson, and it seemed very natural – dust to dust, ashes to ashes. It lasted about five minutes and I poked some crocuses down the side, and there is a tree growing over it. I wanted a place where I could go; and I do go, but not morbidly. I should think I will go about twice a year. I don't want to be morbid about it, but there is also room for my mother there. The stonemason was very sweet and said, 'I don't want to upset you, Madam, but I have left a space at the bottom if you would like to have your mother's name put there.' Although she wasn't particularly interested then, she is now very pleased and she has been up there twice and she likes to feel that one day she will be there.

Afterwards I expected to be much more upset than I was, but I'm sure that my other experience of losing my friend did prepare me, although it was a long time ago and not so close. I didn't feel any guilt at all about my father, I didn't feel that I had left anything unsaid that I ought to have said so I felt quite happy about that. But I do miss him, I miss him terribly. There are always things that I want to tell him. I dread losing my mother: I can't make comparisons between whom I am most fond of, and I do grieve for my father a lot, but I just dread losing my mother. I still dream about my father, and I also have a recurrent dream where my mother, sister, brother and myself are looking for a new home, and father isn't with us. I recently had one very distressing dream about him, he was standing there and I went up to him and put my arm round him and said 'You're not dead after all: oh, good!' When I woke up I was dreadfully upset because he was so real in the dream.

One thing I found very distressing, and still do, was when I went home for the first time afterwards. It upset me terribly that he wasn't there: I kept looking at his desk. I kept looking round all the time, expecting to see him coming in. And there was this strange smell in the house when he was dying; I don't know whether it was cancer or whether it was disinfectant – it was a cloying, sickly smell, like slightly decaying hyacinths, and it was very strong in the house when he was dying. The first time I went back the smell hit me, and my sister noticed it too. It's nearly gone now, but still once or twice I get whiffs of it, and it brings it all back terribly. Smell is the most evocative thing of all: it has so many associations.

The worst shock was when I first knew that he had cancer: I wasn't told, I knew. I took one look at him and I was very, very upset then. That was the worst moment. And after that we were really waiting for him to die. Then there was relief when he actually died – I don't think I have cried much about it at all since. James cries occasionally: he cried last week in the bath when we were listening to 'Songs of Praise': father and I both loved hymns and James said, 'I'm crying for Grandad,' so we had a little talk about heaven and so on. I'm not a conventional church-goer although I do go to church. Funnily enough, the Church of England, of which I am a member and an extremely critical one, the way it handles death and burial is one of its strongest points. It doesn't cope with life nearly as well as it does with death. If you read the funeral service in the 1662 prayer book, there are some of the finest words in the English language. My mother is very religious and has got tremendous comfort from it: one of the last things my father said to my mother before he died was, 'You and I are rolled up together in a ball, I feel as if we were entwined.' And that gave her such courage because she is convinced of a spiritual afterlife. I feel too that my father left his body and he had made up his mind to go: that's why he called his family while he could. The fact that he knew I was there at the end has given me tremendous comfort because I couldn't bear to think he didn't know I was there. I'm not 100 per cent sure of the afterlife, but my mother is quite sure, and quite serene about it.

Having been on tranquillizers for quite a time after my husband left me, it took me a long time to get off them after my father died. I had a very good doctor who didn't try to get me off them quickly, because he knows me well: nor does he just dish out drugs. I was just getting myself off all my pills when my father became ill, and it set me back a bit. It was a minor setback: I'm off them now. In many ways I'm extremely happy for my father, because I think it was what he wanted. I suppose really I mourn for myself and my mother. It's purely selfish, really, I just didn't want him to go. I miss him. Your parents are people who've always been there, and the only people who love you despite your faults. They say that you never grow up until you have lost both your parents and I think it's probably true.

It was right for all of us that we all knew that my father was dying: some people don't want to know, and put up defence mechanisms, but everybody is different. You can't say that my parents' way was better, although I think it was in fact easier: but lots of people are afraid of upsetting each other too much by having it out in the open, and they put on a brave face to avoid the distress.

My mother was exhausted afterwards: she did very well and coped marvellously with all the washing and the nursing, and she seemed fine, but then she was very ill for about three months with flu and acute sinusitis and was in bed for weeks: it was her way of reacting. Now she is doing all sorts of positive things and has picked up a lot – she has thrown herself in almost too much. She made a list of the positive advantages of my father's death; they were very happily married, and like everyone else they had their ups and downs, but he was very loyal to her and they were married for forty-seven years. Although he was very much an intellectual, he loved sport, so she used to hate Saturday afternoons; and she put that down as a bonus that she didn't have to have sport all Saturday afternoon. She finds mealtimes more flexible, as he was getting rather set in his ways. He was hopeless with small children and never really enjoyed his grandchildren: mother likes to pretend that he did, but she knows he didn't and that it's much easier without him. He found them irritating and noisy and they made a mess, and this is a criticism that I can make of him because I don't feel guilty about him. It's sad that he had nine grandchildren and didn't see them at the age when he would have most enjoyed them. My mother finds that she needs to paint a rosy picture of him, but I don't. But otherwise he was a tolerant, gentle person and he was wise: he got a little bit more reactionary in his views as he got older, but he was a very gentle person.

When I got home again after the funeral I didn't feel, 'Oh, dear, I'm all alone, I haven't got a shoulder to cry on,' because although there was a time when my husband and I had been happy, he was absolutely no support to me at the times that I was distressed. I had more sympathy from a close girl-friend, and one or two other friends. I remember coming back and looking at the newly-decorated hall and living-room and thinking, 'Oh, dear, father will never see this,' but of course the reality is that if father had been there he would have been exhausted by the children; I do try to be realistic about it.

I have got a cigarette lighter of his and I have got the cigarette case that I gave him which I carry in my handbag. I've got some of his favourite books. I haven't got as many letters as I would like to have because unfortunately in the last few years, like everybody else, we used the telephone. I carry photographs, some of which upset me sometimes because he was beginning to get ill and it was beginning to show. You can see it coming, and although he was so thin, there is something different there, and it was obviously the beginnings of cancer. There is almost a kind of sadness, and he doesn't look physically fit. I shouldn't carry those ones, I should carry the nice one because that comforts me. One night I couldn't sleep and I came down and looked across at it, and for the first time the eyes were laughing at me and saying, 'I'm alright.' I felt comforted by the picture: I don't find his possessions as comforting as I would have thought – at first I did with the lighter, I thought it was rather nice to feel that I was putting my thumb where he put his, but that feeling seems to have worn off: I feel a bit disloyal about that. Yet you can't go on sustaining that emotion any more than you can sustain the emotion of being in love; you can't live like that. Right at the beginning of grief you will feel it very intensely, and then it changes, it mellows.

I had a lot of very nice letters. Something I haven't been

able to do is to read the great file of letters at home: there are some beautiful letters and I have twice attempted to read them and both times I have broken down and cried, and haven't been able to read them. I want to, but I can't bring myself to; I'm not ready yet. One of my regrets is that we didn't write a tribute for him to be published in *The Times*: I was too upset at the time and too involved in other things, to write it myself or to get anyone else to write one. I do regret that bitterly. The other thing that upset me terribly was that they got the death notice wrong, they made stupid mistakes, and I found that terribly distressing. I still feel cross about it. There is nothing you can do and it is a very bad area to make a mistake in; the moment's passed and you can never put it right.

My mother finds that she wanted to stay on in the house, and she wanted to sleep in the bedroom. I thought she might want to change rooms, but it was very strange – she wanted his bed out of the room immediately, but she wanted to sleep on the mattress on which he died, and she does still. There were two beds very close together and she has got two mattresses on one bed. I still find the actual place where his bed was, where there is now a table and a photograph of him, very distressing. Just occasionally, six months later, I was able to pass the room without looking in and thinking of seeing my father, but on the whole that's the one place where I stop and look. If my mother's in bed and I go in and kiss her goodnight, I have to stand where his bed was and I don't like that; it upsets me still.

Children are marvellous in these situations. James was fantastic: he was very wise and I remember how he behaved at the funeral and how he took it all in and the things he said afterwards. He kept looking at me as we were singing the hymns to see if I was alright. He has said things to me since about Father being in heaven; he says, 'He's alright, he's probably watching football by now, or perhaps he is having a glass of sherry, or a strawberry yoghurt,' little things like that. When the crunch comes, children rally. When my husband left my doctor told me I was in a state of shock and that I must go home and tell James immediately. He was four and a bit, but he said, 'You will find that he takes it like a man and that he will help you.' And he did, at that age: he was absolutely wonderful and he still is. Even if it's their first encounter with death, they seem to react instinctively. They seem to have a kind of maturity and wisdom that adults don't have: out of the mouths of babes and sucklings ... James' whole attitude when he saw my father ill for the first time, and knew he was dying, was remarkable: he hates kissing, but he walked straight up to my father and kissed him on the cheek: I think he knew. When I put him to bed that night he said, 'Is Grandad going to get better?' and I said, 'No,' and he said, 'Is he going to die?' and I said, 'Yes, I'm afraid so.' It was uncanny, yet he was so open and honest about it too. From that time on he kissed him every time he saw him. It'll help him in his experience of life, to accept death in such a natural way. The little girls across the road were shut off from it: my friend made the mistake of not telling the six-year-old that her grandfather had died, and she adored him. He has been dead a year, and she just has not told her. The children were left at home for the funeral and they became very disturbed. She thought I was very peculiar taking James to the funeral, but I know I was right. If you treat children in a grown up way, they will act like grown ups.

11

ALAN:
his father

Alan is a family doctor in a county town, and is married to Sarah who is also a doctor. They are both thirty-five and have three young sons. Alan has an elder brother who lives in Australia and a younger brother who, like him, lives in England: they were all brought up in Kenya. Two years ago Alan's father died of a heart attack after several months of bad health. He was sixty-one and a general practitioner in Nairobi. Alan's mother was fifty-six when he died, and has since moved to England.

And come he slow, or come he fast,
It is but Death who comes at last.

Sir Walter Scott

I knew that my father was unfit. I knew that something would give but I didn't think that he would die. I was very close to him, although there were things that he did that annoyed me. Ever since I was a child he was fairly ruthless in enforcing his rules; I suppose we were quite strictly brought up – not like Quakers and not church-going – but rules were rules, and he was annoying at times. In fact just before he died, the last time I saw him, we went to a pub together. We drove: we could have walked but I don't think he could have made it without having to stop. He started on about my sister-in-law – he's always gone on about our wives. For some reason he didn't seem to get on with his daughters-in-law. I hadn't seen him for a long time, and we were in this pub, and he started to go on about her; I thought, 'I can't stand this any more.' Up to then we had let him get away with it because he was the ruler of the family: he ruled the roost as it were, but I really thought it was about time somebody said, 'Look, shut up, we're fed up with this.' So I said my piece: I said, 'We're fed up to the back teeth, all three of us, if you'd like to know, with hearing nothing but criticism of our wives.' That shook him a bit; I was obviously a bit sorry and said so. He said, 'No, fair enough,' and seemed to be able to take it alright. He went off home to Kenya and then a letter came saying, 'Don't worry about that episode.' He hadn't written me a letter for three or four years I should think. It was a super letter; very short, very nice. 'You had a point to make and you made it. No hard feelings'. Chitter chatter, chitter chatter. About a fort-night after that he died. He seemed to know, somehow.

We weren't fighting all the time. I might have given the impression that we got on like tom cats, but far from it. Certainly I wished he would stop smoking and he wouldn't. I wished he'd go for a walk and he wouldn't. I wished he'd stop drinking and he wouldn't; so we had a lot of niggling differences between us. He was never really polite about my children: my elder brother's eldest son was the blue-eyed boy and he hardly ever took any notice of my three. That upset Sarah more than it did me: it was unnecessary but it was one of his quirks.

There was at one time a slight suspicion of suicide. The doctor who should have looked after him as he was dying, and who should have looked after Mummy when it all happened, behaved abominably. He was the one who first put the thought of suicide into my mother's head, and obviously it really upset her. But I knew that he was very unwell: his liver was probably only half there and something was going to give, and he died. It came as a shock though, because he hadn't been bedridden or in hospital or under a doctor or anything like that. He died at home and my mum was there with him. The support for her at that time was negligible: the doctor didn't come when he should have; there had been a bit of a feud between him and my father but that was no reason why he shouldn't look after the situation when it actually came to a head. It was he who suggested a post mortem, and that's what really upset my mother: he wasn't prepared to sign a death certificate to start with, so he had a post mortem. It was proved to be a myocardial infarct, but I don't know how good the laboratory was, and having got an answer like that it wasn't worth unravelling any more.

I first heard that he had died when my mother phoned from Kenya. It was lunchtime and we were just about to go away for the weekend. I knew something was terribly wrong, and she said it straight out. She was obviously very worried that I was going to fall off the phone: I think that doing it by telephone is the worst possible way. It should not be done by telephone, it should be done by the policeman coming to the door. Not that I've had a policeman coming to the door but at least you've got a human being there. I once did it as a doctor by phone and the person fell off at the other end. It was horrific. However, I'm sure she did the right thing to phone me because of the distance involved – and who else could she tell? Well, I managed to hang on to the phone and talk about it. I asked how it had happened and how she was and then I tried fairly hard to be practical about it. Who else had she phoned? Who did she want to come out? Only by being practical could I actually keep my emotions out of it. One couldn't keep one's emotions out of it, let's face it. She must have been able to hear from the wobbling voice and all sorts of things that I wasn't faring particularly well. But I sorted out who I had to phone, I arranged that she had her best friend there and that she was going to spend the night out of the house with her, and that I would phone her back to tell her which of us was coming out to Kenya – I suppose mainly to look after my mum, but also I suppose in a silly way out of respect for my father, that one of us would actually be present at his burial.

By this time Sarah had come in and knew immediately what had happened. I can't remember how the conversation came to an end but I said, 'Cheerio,' in a wobbly kind of voice and collapsed in a heap of convulsing sobbing. I was rather surprised at my reaction after having had the biff with my father, although I don't think there was any remorse over the episode in the pub; none whatever. I didn't feel that at all because it was an episode finished. After a considerable while I simmered down and set about the business of phoning my brothers to tell them what had happened.

I went out to Kenya for the funeral. I'm very glad I did. I didn't see him after his death: I went out fully intending to, partly because of what I tell people to do as a doctor, and partly because I thought it might help me too. I twice said, 'I ought to go and see Daddy after he's died,' and my mum said, 'Look, it's a tropical country, he's had a post mortem and you've no idea what he'll look like. Far from looking serene and at peace, it may well be a dreadful shock. Have another think about it.' Then by tea-time I said, 'I think I really ought to go and see Daddy,' because I had gone out having decided to. I could have done, she wasn't forceful, but she said it again: in essence that it was two days and she didn't know whether he had been refrigerated, although she didn't use those words. So I didn't see my father. It doesn't worry me too much. I know what he looked like and if I shut my eyes I can see him, the way he was before he died.

The burial was like a Graham Greene novel. Not very many people came, but the people who did come came from a long way away. An Indian was arranging it all with an Indian-made coffin and all that sort of thing. All these Africans were going to carry the coffin from the little pedestal where the service is, to where it was laid to rest. I can't remember the last funeral I went to – I think it was the cremation of my step-grandfather – so I hadn't even looked at a prayer book to see what the rigmarole was. I didn't know whether you gathered all the flowers up at the end or chucked them into the grave, or when you sprinked the dust in, or whether the priest did or I did. I had no idea. But I went around and got five fairly strong people so that we could carry the coffin ourselves. It was very heavy. Opposite me was a chap I had grown up with who's as strong as an ox, so I felt safe opposite him. They put the ropes underneath and as we let it down, one of the little tinny handles flew off. I mean, what can you do? I suppose if I went through it again I would have gone to the Indian and said, 'Let's have a look at the coffin,' and I wouldn't have let them put the ropes through the handles. If they'd put them just under the coffin so that it was slung, it would have been perfectly alright, but they put them through the handles so that as you pulled apart they just pinged off, and the coffin lurched down. It really was like a Graham Greene novel turned into a film. I just hope my mum was alright. Anyway, it didn't crash to the bottom – we just held on and looked at each other and let it down to the bottom and that was that. He's buried in a place where he would have liked to be buried; although he wasn't one of the original colonials, he'd become one, and there he is under a mango tree in Mombasa.

Subsequently I would say that for me the bereavement was very easy. I don't know why: I knew what to expect, a little bit. Obviously, never having been in the same shoes you can never possibly tell what it may be like, but I had some idea of what my mother would go through. In fact, I think that because I was so concerned about how Mummy was then, I didn't have to worry about myself any more. I had a few more cries about it; we talked about it quite a lot, my mum and I. I was the only one out there for the funeral and to begin with, then my eldest brother came out and overlapped with me, and then my younger brother came out and over-lapped with him. So my mum had one of us around for the next five weeks or so. She must have talked a lot to both of them, and she also talked an awful lot to me. I suppose in some ways I took over his role, for my mother. I've never thought before of that being what helped me through, but now I'm sure it did. Without that it would have been very very different. I'm sure it was the greatest help there was, and still is, that I am looking after my mother.

One thing we managed to do, and I can't remember whether it was my idea or not, although I may have in-fluenced the decision, and that was to have a kind of wake. I don't know how I believed in it or why I believed in it, but we thought we should have a wake. After the prayers and the burial we asked everyone who was still going to be in Mombasa round for tea, and I said, 'When we get around to having tea we're going to open a few bottles because the sad bit is finished and we're going to have a good old chinwag.' It went like a bomb. It's an awful thing to say, but it went very well. It was terribly easy and my mum was very pleased that we'd done it; she'd had the idea that people were coming for tea basically for her to be able to thank them for coming, but we opened the bottles up and it worked: not that the alcohol did it, but the fact that it was a happier time. There were people there for her to chat to that she hadn't seen for weeks or months or even years.

I tend to think that my mum believes he's in heaven; I think she does and it may be terribly important to her. I don't, personally. I haven't even actually thought that when I die I'll go to heaven and see my father there. I don't believe he's anywhere. The only place he is, is the effect that he has had on me: all the goodness that has come from him shows in lots of things that I do. I don't dream much anyway so I can't say I've dreamed about him.

Perhaps I can be technical about this: I can see it from a professional angle even though I myself am involved. I had a grief reaction, definitely. I can't put it in terms of duration because one is emerging from it all the time, gradually, so how can you say when it ends? But it didn't affect my work – if anything it helped my work because before I had had the experience of the death of a close relative, how could I handle someone else's bereavement? It's pathetic, really, how one is expected to, not knowing how they feel and not having had any training in bereavement. But now I find it much easier to handle. In terms of a grief reaction, it certainly didn't affect my appetite, my sleep, or my functioning in any way. Without a doubt it helped me to talk about it: as we emerged from the sadness of it all, it gradually unwound and one would talk less about it. I was not that emotionally disturbed by it that often: in a matter of weeks I was over it. Although insomnia is 100 per cent expected I hardly suffered from it at all. The discussions that went on about it helped; they were mainly with my mother and we talked about the good that he'd put into life, because latterly it had been a bit forgotten. He was drinking more and smoking more, and it

117

tended to discolour the years and years of good that he'd put in to looking after people.

It has affected me inasmuch as it has increased my understanding: I know a bit more what other people are feeling. It's made me a better doctor, I hope: I think it has helped enormously. When one of my patients dies I go through it with ease whereas before I felt such an imposter, because I hadn't lost any relatives. I don't know that it's done much more than that to my personality. Compared to most people's, mine is a very dull bereavement, luckily for me. I'm very grateful that it doesn't affect me and that there have been a lot of things that have contributed to it being that way: the fact that he was ill; that I had my mother to look after, which has been my prime objective.

Back here in England friends were very sympathetic. I don't remember anybody doing a sort of, 'Gee, I'm sorry,' sort of noise. If anybody was in the least bit awkward I was already better by a fortnight afterwards and I was able to get rid of their awkwardness. People don't know what to say when someone's lost a close relative: it just happens to be fashionable at the moment not to say, 'Gee, I'm sorry.' On the other hand, if someone says it and it's the only thing they can think of saying, you feel that it's meant, and that they are otherwise at a loss for words. No, people were fine. In fact it was my partner who said that I must go to Kenya: he said, 'Your mother's on her own out there and you've got to go.' I said, 'Well, there's all the work here, and it's all unplanned.' But he wouldn't let me beat about the bush and he was right. The workload at the time was terribly heavy, but they managed.

It has confirmed my instinctive feelings about ritual. The wake is important. Seeing the body can be important. I don't know why and I don't know what any of these beliefs are based on. I think they must be based on what the wild Irish do and what the wild Kikuyu do. Both cultures have a pattern of how to get over it, they have a system: the Irish have a wake and the Kikuyu have a great wail which goes on for two or three days, getting more and more glassy-eyed as it goes on. It is through rituals that they do get over it. Rituals matter. I think that seeing the body after death is terribly important because I have experienced the disbelief in other people. They don't believe the person is dead, they have a sense of unreality about it until they have seen with their own eyes. The only thing that holds them back from seeing the body is a fear that it looks awful after death, whereas in fact, most times – and there are obvious exceptions – it looks fantastic, particularly after an illness. I think that if it's a sudden death the difference between the pink of health and the greyness of death is a bit more sombre. But certainly after a gruelling illness: I still find it remarkable when I see the peace on the face, the lack of worry lines. I go back to the relatives and say to them that they really must see the person now because he wasn't like this yesterday. He looked frightful yesterday and now he looks fine: he really looks as if he hasn't got a care in the world. I encourage them – not force them – by saying, 'I think you ought to go through and say goodbye.'

The other thing is that even when somebody is obviously dead, the family sometimes don't seem to know it. One really absurd thing that happens is that the ambulance drivers get called out and when they arrive, the person is dead: they are not allowed to actually say that the person is dead. So they have to sit there, knowing he's dead, until a doctor arrives who is allowed to say, 'He's dead.' There may be some sense in it somewhere but it's a fact that in the middle of the night there will be two ambulance drivers hanging around for me to pitch up and say, 'Yes, he's dead.' Often the relatives are all in the room and there he is, stone dead, and they don't realise it. I have to speak to the next of kin, alone usually. I say, 'I'm afraid he's died,' or words to that effect – I never know what I'm going to say until I've said it. I suppose one should leave out the 'I'm afraid' because I'm *not* afraid, but it's just the way one speaks. Often – and this always used to surprise me – they then say, 'Oh, he hasn't, has he?'; and yet he's been there, obviously dead, for half an hour or even longer. The little switch won't turn on until the doctor comes and says, 'He's dead.' So the major reason for them to go in and see that he's died is to make it real to them. Particularly after sudden deaths when it's unexpected, although it's important in both situations. With unexpected death it's much harder to get them to agree to the idea of death. The disbelief is much harder to conquer.

Medically, I see bereavement as fairly straightforward. I may be wrong, but I feel very strongly that it's like patching houses, it's like architecture to an extent. Once upon a time, not so very long ago, they knew a hell of a lot more about it. They talked more about it, they were more aware of it and they managed it all very well. The Victorians were right into ritual: possibly it was the First World War that killed that off, when there was such mass slaughter. I know it's also a question of fashion: personally I don't want to be driven round the town in a big hearse at two miles an hour, but too much of that ritual has gone: like so many things that we did know an awful lot about, we have forgotten it: it's lost knowledge. We live in an age of mass production and so we die in mass production.

12

DUNCAN:
both his parents

*Duncan and Fran are both forty and now live in his parents'
old home in a village. They have three young children,
Louisa, Owen and Jo. Four years ago his parents, aged sixty-
four and sixty-eight, were killed in a car smash on the
motorway: an empty furniture van was blown across the
barrier and crashed over their car. Duncan heard the news
over the phone in New York where he was working for a
branch of his father's company. Since then he has returned to
live in his childhood home and retired from the company,
choosing to convert his inherited land in Scotland into a
profit-making concern.*

'Tis held that sorrow makes us wise.

Tennyson: *In Memoriam*

Duncan: The facets of this bereavement thing open up a kind
of chain reaction: a 'decision tree'. They cause a whole series
of things to react and interact until you end up with a whole
explosion of events that end up a long way from those two
people lying in their box ten feet under. There are frustra-
tions, problems that arise due to silly decisions, or jealousies,
or lack of frankness. You get the interesting aspect of how in-
laws react: some sons-in-law or daughters-in-law suddenly
become rapacious and grasping; others have a completely
different reaction: 'I don't want to know, I really don't want
anything to do with it at all,' neither of which are responsible.

You need to bring it into the centre, to be able to talk, not necessarily rationally, but at least commercially about it. All these things arise as a result of termination; people, in spite of having a lot of experience – because people die all the time – don't seem to pass the wisdom on very well. Perhaps because the person making the will has their own personal idiosyncrasies anyway, and also maybe the loss is the first time around for the people involved, that the problems arise; they come out of their lack of experience.

I was abroad when my parents were killed, and I heard it over the telephone. I got a phone call, and the person telling me was my boss. I could tell he was having difficulty on the other end of the phone and I could hear a sense of urgency in the voice. He said, 'Look, are you on your own?' and I said, 'Yes,' and he said, 'Your parents have been in a car smash.' I said to him, 'Are they dead?' – I just asked him straight out and he said, 'Well, as things are at the moment we are not sure.' So I said, 'So you are saying that they are as good as dead, or dying?' and he said, 'Yes.' I said, 'Well thanks very much for telling me and let me get back to you.' It was short and not even very factual, and I hung up.

The first confrontation with someone was the one that was most difficult, but it had to happen: it was with my colleague, my number two. I called him on the intercom and said, 'Could you come and see me please?' and he said, 'I'm a bit busy at the moment,' and I said, 'Well it really is rather important,' so he came in. He sat down and I said, 'Look, things aren't too good, you'll just have to bear with me for a moment,' and he said, 'God Almighty, what's happened?' and I said, 'Just let me count ten,' and I just managed to cope with that and we sat there and you could see on his face, 'Oh, Lord, I know what he's going to tell me. I wonder who it is – is it his wife, or children?' And there was I and I couldn't get it out and eventually I said, 'Look, I'm sorry,' and I started to cry and I said, 'My parents have been killed in a car crash,' and poor fellow, he practically fainted. I can see him now, he just sat on the edge of his chair and it was as though I had wired him up and said, 'Are you ready for it?' and then pressed the button.

He just sat there; we both sat like a couple of dummies. All my hair was standing on end, like I'd had a thousand volts. He said, 'Oh God, I just don't know what to say,' and I said, 'Well, there is nothing to say. What we have got to do is to get the show on the road. Now obviously I think the first thing is, could you tell the office and let everyone know so there is no problem there.' There must have been about twenty-eight people there, all different ethnic groups – the New York scene – and when I walked out it was like a wailing wall. It was amazing. There was I, slightly red-eyed, doing my British stiff-upper-lip bit: 'Now come on, toughen yourself up.' My secretary, who is a middle-aged spinster, had mascara pouring down her face and I said, 'Look, come on, it can't be that bad.' And of course they couldn't believe that I was behaving normally. I don't know what they expected me to do, pass out or something; I suppose I was shocked. She just put her hands on her head and practically fell over and I said, 'Now, come on, it's not that bad, like the old goody crow, it has to go sometime.'

Then there was the question of telling Fran; I rang her and she said, 'Look, I'm busy, I can't talk to you now,' and I got furious on the phone and said, 'God, Christ Almighty, I have got a message to tell you, woman, I'm coming home and I want you to be there.' 'Oh, what's happened?' 'I'll tell you when I get back, now for God's sake give me a break': I got really aggressive with her and when I got home, she, knowing something was wrong, opened the door and I just said, 'Wait for it and I'll tell you in a minute.' Then I told her. She was terribly supportive.

By that time the first sort of bang was over – like when someone hits you very hard: once you pick yourself up and shake yourself down, then you get going. I found a whole series of things to do and say, like, 'We have to look after the children and we have to tell them what it's about.' There is a whole chain of events that makes you have to think things out. There was a quasi-business situation and of course there was the family. I spoke to both my sisters in England; I phone them and they said, 'Oh, good, thanks for phoning; now look, you're not to worry, everything is under control.' It was as though all of us had galvanised ourselves and so it was terribly business-like: there was no wailing over the phone. I said, 'How are you coping?' 'Oh, OK, but you know it's early days yet.' Both of them are terribly sensible.

I think the only thing that I didn't look forward to, so my brother-in-law did it, was to go and identify the bodies. I was quite glad to be out of that. He said they were terribly peaceful in the mortuary. As long as they are not too mutilated, what they generally do for identification purposes is just show you the face and they do tidy the person up a bit. They might be a bit bruised but they look peaceful and asleep. I don't spend much time in mortuaries so I can't claim to have seen many corpses: it has its moments of humour, of course.

I found it quite hard talking about it to people I didn't know, and I found it difficult to talk to people who I did know without crying or feeling uncomfortable just wanting to cry. I don't mind crying and so I would shed a tear: it's rather a good sort of sympathy thing – at least people offer you a drink!

Anyway, we sat down and I said to Fran, 'The children will sense it,' so we went to tell the children. Of course we had been away for quite a few years and grandparents to them were just an idea, they weren't real: they didn't have a relationship with them. Louisa was six, Owen was four and Jo was eight. We sat down and I started to talk and once I was telling them they sat there looking absolutely sweet. I shed a tear and Louisa, I think it was, said, 'Dad, why are you crying?' and I said, 'Well, it's sad you know, because they were my mum and dad and they have been killed in a car smash, and it's just one of those things. They didn't suffer.' Owen said something like, 'I promise to very good while you're away' – like a little man – and then Louisa said, 'I know why you've got to go back to England,' so we said 'Why?' and she said, 'You gotta go and get the bones.' It sort of released the tension of it – we just laughed until we ached. It was so sweet, absolutely divine.

Then the chain of events started. It was funny how people became terribly shocked as they found out. By this time I was in the phase of, 'Come on, we have got to get on with it: let's get packed and put a black tie in,' and that sort of thing. As the ripple effect gathered, so the drama gathered gradually, and so instead of saying, 'Let's ring up so and so to have the children,' we had to cope with twenty-five people ringing up and saying, 'Can we help?' You don't want to sound ungrateful but you are coping with all sorts of barriers that are being put up, and forming defence mechanisms; meanwhile people are dropping in and it's overwhelming.

I came to England a day or so in advance and it was great, seeing my sisters. They were both terribly calm about it. There was just the question of getting everything organised. All that funeral bit, it's done for you – I mean you just press a button and say you want a Grade I or whatever it is, and all those guys with black hats and things turn up and do the right thing.

But characteristic of my family I suppose, my sisters and I were terribly conscious of putting on a very good show so it should be a super funeral. And it was, it was really rather enjoyable. We were terribly proud of the way we did it. Both my sisters weren't too sure, either of them, how they were going to cope, but we had great confidence in each other and Deborah took the excuse to go and buy some wildly expensive outfit, and they looked absolutely fabulous. Deborah is a couple of years older than me and Belinda three or four years younger.

We had the family here for lunch and we said to the caterer, 'We'd better have fresh salmon and we want home-made mayonnaise and champagne.' We had an enormous lunch because we have got a large family and they all turned up: we'd said 'no mourning and no flowers' and they all turned up looking rather uncertain of what was going to take place, but within half an hour it was as if a great party was going on. It was fun to see them all again, not that we are a terribly close family, but thousands of cousins got in on the act. We said 'no flowers' because my father said my mother didn't like that sort of thing. In fact my father had a rather amusing codicil to his will: he said, 'I would like the service to be: no mourning, no flowers and the service to be as cheerful as possible, commensurate with the policies of my less serious-minded relatives'; which was rather sweet.

The whole village closed down for the day. It has quite a big church which was packed to the gunnels and more. We had wonderful readings, some of them from Indian philosophical writings, and the service was done with a certain panache. Then everyone was invited back here afterwards. The caterer at the end practically ran out of booze: he said, 'Good God, you have consumed more than people consume at most weddings,' and we thought, 'Well, that's a good send-off, that's what Mother and Dad would have liked.' Father was a great party man.

After that there comes the let-down, when it's all done; and then you start getting the will and everything sorted out. In retrospect I think the problems over that were probably very small. There were some interpretation problems, there was a suppressed feeling of, 'Well, I think that's a pretty odd way to do it,' and this sort of thing – it wasn't clear, because neither parent had really thought it through since they didn't expect to die. I think I can say I wasn't threatened by my sisters at all on it until I felt that my brothers-in-law were getting in on the act. They were saying, 'Well I think we should have this,' and, 'Why should they have that?' and both my sisters were really quite firm with them. To their credit they turned around and said, 'Mind your own business.' But often that's where the fun tends to start.

I stayed here for about a month and Fran went back. There was the memorial service to organise, then there was the looking to the detail and working out how the estate should be carved up. There was no time for thinking about grief at that stage: it's amazing how quickly you settle down. Very sensibly we were both given some sleeping pills and some valium and I think I took them for a couple of weeks until I started to get a good night's sleep again and got into a good sleep routine again.

Fran: You had quite a reaction after the funeral and before the memorial service: you got flu and you couldn't attend the memorial service.

Duncan: True; but whether that was anything to do with the death or not I don't know. The crying goes on for a long time: that depends on how surprised you are. If someone gives you a big surprise and you're not ready for it then it will produce a tear. I remember for instance feeling quite surprised when friends were here the other weekend and the husband cross-questioned me quite aggressively and I felt quite emotional at one point, didn't you?

Fran: Yes; one isn't used to being asked a direct question of have you got over your parents' death, even three years later.

Duncan: I remember when we were staying in France someone showed us a cine film of their holiday and suddenly Mum and Dad walked on the screen and he obviously heard me gasp because I wasn't ready for it. Even now, going through photograph albums, if I come across a picture of my parents that I'm not used to seeing, there is always a little jump.

Fran: The getting-over takes a very long time; to get immune.

Duncan: I had actually spent some time when I first came back from America discussing who we should sue, but obviously you can't sue anyone: driving into other people and killing them, you don't. I feel no bitterness towards the driver; but it was an extraordinary case because the man had been warned three times not to go on driving – it was in high winds – and Counsel said that we might win the case but we wouldn't get more than nominal damages. That's the way we look at damages in this country.

Fran: I think your work was rather a release for you, afterwards, because it absorbed you and took your mind off things.

Duncan: And I'm a conventionally religious person; I go to church but I don't think about God. I suppose I believe they're somewhere else but when I go and throw bread to the swans I don't think I'm giving Mum a second bite of a crust or anything. I don't have a strong feeling of an afterlife, it's something that I feel personally is a waste of time thinking about. There is no answer to it: I'm a person who likes to get on with life. I'm an ambitious man and there are a lot of factual things to get hold of without wondering what's going on down there. It doesn't worry me one way or the other. Death is a fact. Sometimes when I'm in the churchyard mowing the grass and I drive near their grave I wonder what they are doing down there, but more in a humorous way than anything else.

Fran: Your mother was killed outright according to the inquest report, which I found very upsetting to read actually. I made myself read it because I thought it was necessary.

Duncan: I'll tell you what was really spooky: when we got back to America there was a letter from my mother that was posted the morning that she had been killed. We opened it and that gave us a bit of a jump.

Fran: I find that the more I come into contact with death as an adult, the less I believe in religion, perhaps because of the violence of the death. I mean in God the Father, the Son, and the Holy Ghost part of it. I respect the fact that it's there, and that there is a church, and I think the need is very great for the convention of a funeral after death. It is painful to go through but I think it is a very necessary ritual. This hasn't given me a wider mystic or spiritual belief either; it's worked the other way for me. I was brought up very much in the church and I want to believe unquestioningly, but I do question more and more as I get older, which I feel sad about. I wish I didn't.

Duncan: I think about death much more. I think about it in relation to relationships. I drive up and down to Scotland quite a lot so we pass the gap in the road where it happened and I often think about it. I selfishly think that I'd much rather die first because I couldn't cope with running this house and the children. Nor the grief.

Fran: Actually, your emotional outlet is crying, isn't it? Duncan cries very easily.

Duncan: I could tell a story to people – a sad one – or read it, and not only reduce myself but also the audience to tears. Very easily. If I were to read *The Snow Goose* to the children I would get them all crying and myself as well.

Fran: Whereas I don't necessarily bottle it up, but I don't cry easily. I'm not as emotional as you, outwardly.

Duncan: I talked to Fran a lot about my parents and the

accident and their lives. Endlessly. But I found some relief in their death, too. One of the big problems we have in society is this question of geriatrics. In the old days you lived your threescore years and ten and that was it, but now because it is regarded as a sort of advance in western civilisation we try to keep people alive long after they are serving any useful purpose to the community or frequently to themselves. I think you can see how a lot of families have their development arrested by always having to look after someone who is infirm, because nobody does it well. The state doesn't do it, and even if they did, who wants to die that way, in hospital?

The fabric of society has been broken up, the community is now much more fluid, and the geriatric doesn't fit in, so here we are: there is a paradox that in causing longevity – supposed to be one of the great secrets – we only find that it causes a great block at the other end. Both my parents had reasonably good health and they were on the whole fit and active, and they were looking forward to retirement. But there was this nagging feeling of what they were actually going to do when they retired – if you look at retirement it is a sinister thing. It's like an abyss to a lot of people who have worked all their lives and arbitrarily are told at the age of sixty-five to get off the train. You hope it's standing still and that the platform's there, but for a lot of people it's not. A lot of people make behavioural noises of what they are going to do when they retire but frequently they wither on the vine and literally die because their self esteem and their motivation disappear. I had all sorts of doubts about them, knowing them well. And both of them were quite difficult, without knowing it.

Fran: One interesting thing that I have never found in any other family is how strong the reaction against their parents was when they were adult. I certainly haven't known any other family so well, and I found it quite shocking to start with although I am used to it now. The three children are all very strong personalities, which is fortunate because their parents were very strong personalities. There was an enormous familiarity and communication with their parents in one sense, but in another, they sometimes did say, 'Well, it will be easier when they are dead.'

Duncan: I was actually relieved when my mother died. She was very difficult.

Fran: I think you may have conditioned yourself to this way of thinking, to a certain extent, but they were very much alike and she bullied all her children very much.

Duncan: But I wouldn't be bullied and I fought. For years I never went home.

Fran: And it was lucky, because they would have all been weak people if they had let her sit on them. Their defence was to try to be stronger than she was, and fight back. Duncan and his younger sister particularly always had a feeling of inadequacy when they were around her, and so, in a sense, her death was a relief for them. Yet in another way there was a sort of going off the rails as well, although not for Duncan, and I think that I could say absolutely objectively. That's because I'm here with him and we have a very good marriage. But where Belinda is concerned, she had six children almost in defiance of her mother, who was always going on about how nobody should have more than 2.5 children, and her marriage broke up afterwards. Then she had a mental problem, and the reaction from friends is that if her mother hadn't died it would never have happened and she would never have left her husband. I think the marriage would have gone on, albeit unhappily. Few people will admit that there is almost a release in their parent's death unless it is someone they have been nursing for a long time. But in this case it was a sudden, completely unexpected event.

Duncan: It changed my role because of the business relationship – as soon as my father died my power-base disappeared, just like that.

Fran: I think it changed Duncan as a person. Rather to his sisters' chagrin, he took on the role of head of the family very quickly and in a very organised way, partly because of his business training and also a tremendous sense of responsibility towards his sisters. I was very proud of him for it, but his sisters in a way felt a little resentful about the fact that he was running their lives. It was partly the male progenitor bit –

the fact that he inherited the land and they inherited the goods and chattels, so there was a certain amount of distinction. Stirred perhaps more by my brothers-in-law than by the sisters themselves. But I think it matured Duncan enormously, if I can say this objectively. You've had ups and downs, but you had never had something that had been this close, you hadn't had any real tragedy in your life. Your life had been in comparison with many, a very easy life. It's made you a much more thoughtful and much broader person: you are a much easier person to be married to, because of being a much more understanding person – which is also to do with the fact that you are no longer involved in an essentially very uncreative and frustrating business life.

Duncan: It may seem a hard thing to say, but various very good things have come out of their death. It's like a game of chess: you're locked into a chess board situation and when you move, even pawns become important. Using the chess analogy, we children had all been married for a number of years so the *dramatis personae* started to get the chess board into a set piece in which moves are extremely slow. I had been abroad for five years, so the relationship I had with the figures on the board, my family, was essentially me looking at the chess board rather than being a piece on it. I could see the conflict patterns, and although we corresponded a lot, when the crunch came, I was not part of that chess board; we had our own little chess board. I felt I was much more ready to cope with the whole thing because of the support that Fran had given. The assumption of the role of looking after both my sisters was partly an intuitive one, because both their husbands were incapable of doing so. The house had been offered to me years before, in deference to Fran, because I wasn't getting on with my mother at all yet she was very fond of Fran. It was a sort of help that we had been abroad for five years – we were able to stand back and see the scenario for what it was.

Getting back to the question of relief, I had had some ghastly rows with my mother in my day, involving physical violence at times, in which I made sure that I came off best. I had been fed up for years and years being told I was a failure and really not until I married did I find at all that I could face her with any equanimity. Even then I used to be really quite frightened about meeting her, so the fact that she wasn't there any more meant that a large barrier had been removed.

Fran: Yet the saddest thing was that you had got to know your father on a really good basis only a few years before you went abroad. You did miss him very much and you felt a great sadness in missing the communication that you had started to build up and wished that you could have carried on with.

Duncan: Yet I missed my mother too: she was an enormous personality, and she could be frightfully funny and good company – she was a very interesting person.

Fran: I miss them very much for the sake of the children; I feel that my children should have their grandparents.

When I came over from America for the funeral I found it an extremely lonely experience: I minded yet I didn't mind that Duncan and his sisters had such a close relationship, although they always boasted that they were independent of each other. But they were very dependent on each other for that occasion. I felt very lonely: I don't think I felt left out because I felt it was right that they should be dependent on each other but I felt I was carrying a great grief on my own in a way. I was very fond of her and she was very fond of me in a way, too. She reacted as female to female – her youngest daughter had been very difficult with her. One of the saddest things was when I couldn't help the tears pouring down my face at the funeral and Belinda turned to me afterwards and said, 'I saw you crying,' and I thought, 'What a sad thing.' I'm not ashamed of having cried and it was difficult not to, and in a way she almost wanted to hurt me. It was so sad that she had to be so aggressive about it.

Duncan: Well, she felt very much the same way as I did. Her husband saw my mother as very much the substitute mother and he blubbed like a whale as well. I didn't, actually, at the funeral, it didn't worry me because I knew it was all going to happen. It's only when you're caught by surprise that you can't control yourself.

Fran: I think it was really two or three weeks afterwards that was the most difficult time, when one was no longer having to behave well. The reality struck home after the state of shock.

Duncan: I remember the enormous help that I had from answering all the bereavement letters. I kept them all. There were hundreds and hundreds and I felt sometimes that I was writing to people I didn't know. And the lovely lady who was my first-ever school teacher wrote, and *I* thought she was ninety when she taught *me*!

It was a great relief to go back to New York – we had a kind of anonymity there. They are lovely people there and they were very kind to us. They had no idea of the set up or what my parents were like so we weren't hassled in any way. But later on it wasn't difficult moving back into the house, because the contents were entirely removed.

Fran: This was the condition that we made in a way, which was hard on Duncan's sisters but they did inherit all the goods and chattels, everything that was in the house. I'm not a very definite person about lots of things but I felt very strongly that we could not move in here with things that belonged to them. We moved in literally with packing cases, which did ease it.

One of the things that we inherited was the old house-keeper, who is now seventy-six. She comes up here quite a lot – she came at the age of sixteen as lady's maid and she has been here more or less ever since. Her reaction about Duncan's parents is very interesting in that she believes totally what she wants to believe and she makes up a fantasy world. She will say, 'Mrs. H. spoke to me this morning,' and she has built up a marvellous memory of them which is terrific and a protection for herself, but it's a dream world. And Duncan's father, who never really noticed her even – she will say how he used to go in and talk to her and tell her all sorts of things: maybe it's true but I very much doubt it.

Duncan: In no way do I idealise my parents after their death; we are terrible parent-knockers in our family. I don't think I'm quite such a knocker as my sisters, but my sisters thought they were rather ghastly parents, which on the whole they were: they had no conception of how to bring up children. In fact I had neither a positive or a negative relationship with them until I was about twenty: they were a generation that didn't show that one existed. And yet I grieved for them because from the age of twenty-eight to thirty-six we developed strong intellectual relationships and father started to refer to me on matters of judgement. But the stun of death whether you like or don't like the person is still the same. It didn't matter what they did in the past.

Fran: It's very difficult to be objective about parents. As somebody coming in to the family from outside I thought his parents were fantastic and ideal because they had always been so interesting with their children. They met so many interesting people, and they were even made to drink beer at a young age because it was all a part of growing up. I lived in such a protected background that I never had any of this and yet the three of you were always moving, always meeting politicians and different people who came to the house. They had to converse with people and were taught to debate from a very early age. They were made to speak French at certain meals – and so you weren't neglected really, you were just pushed up to the nursery when you weren't wanted.

Duncan: It's very difficult to evaluate. I am a person who has an enormous capacity as a rule for getting enjoyment out of meagre situations.

I think that the question of avarice versus generosity and acquisitiveness is a problem. There is a theory of course which says that the size of the estate doesn't matter because the relativity of it is what's important and so the little Victorian silver thimble which was Grandmother's and was promised to me and I can't have because it's gone to someone else, can be blown up out of all proportion. In our case there were hundreds and hundreds of items and the amount of probate was enormous, so there was plenty to argue about and I think to be magnanimous about it required an amount of self-discipline. That brought my sisters together because it became clear that both my brothers-in-law had no intention of being magnanimous. Fran on the contrary was extremely sensitive about not wanting to appear rapacious. Luckily, because all the figures were so big, I could say, 'You take the

furniture if that's what you want,' and all three of us were able
to keep the other elements that might have distorted it out of
it. Since then, my elder sister has come to trust my judgement: I am closer to them now, but it has put enormous
pressure on their marriages. Neither of them had a happy
marriage and one has broken up completely and the other
broke up for a while and is now back together again, but it
has been a very lonely time for both of them. But on the
whole there has been no major row.

For us, the repercussions are different: it is a very big
estate, and we could either have thrown it in and sold it, or
done what I'm doing: it's going to cost me money but I
approached it in – well, some people say a foolhardy way,
others say courageous. Time will tell. If it's not a success it
will be foolhardy, if it is a success it will be courageous. It is
said that success has a thousand fathers while failure is an
orphan. The gamble is quite big and it takes me away from
home a lot and I couldn't do it unless I had a stable marriage
and a wife who went along with it, because the supportive-
ness needed is very great. So it's changed my lifestyle inasmuch as I am away from home more than I used to be. That
question of changing is a very difficult one: so many things
apart from their death have happened. You can count that as
an obvious identifiable watershed, when the whole caboose
went over, but so many things now have gone on down the
river that to actually say it's all the result of that watershed is
a bit remote.

13

GORDON:
his wife

Gordon is forty-one and a computer manager for an airline company. Five months ago his wife died of cancer at the age of thirty-seven, six weeks after having been told that she was terminally ill. Gordon is now left with their three children, aged eleven, eight and five.

Man that is born of a woman hath but a short time to live, and is full of misery. He cometh up, and is cut down, like a flower; he fleeth as it were a shadow ... In the midst of life we are in death.

The Book of Common Prayer: Burial Service

We both knew what was happening just before Christmas, and she died towards the end of February. I saw the consultant who had operated on her, and I was warned beforehand by the physician, so by then I knew roughly what was happening. She knew a little while after I did. Obviously it came as a terrible shock, but she took it exceptionally well. She never really broke down at all. That period of knowing that she was dying was a very positive time for us: seeing the way she was taking it and the positive way she was making me look at things, I was forced to look in a positive direction rather than a negative direction. Having three children to look after, you are forced not to worry so much about things that you can't do anything about. She did teach me to be exceptionally constructive in my approach to things and to look at the good points, and not to be defeatist.

We do have paths to tread in life I'm afraid; but there were a number of things around which were there to help. I'm not too prone to depression, but in periods when I might think that things weren't going quite my way, it helps to think of my three children who are there to remind me of her: instead of having a piece of stone as a memorial, I have got three children and that soon gets me over it.

My first reaction when I was told that she was dying was, 'That's life. If it's happened, it's happened.' The only time I cried was on the day of the funeral, and then not very much, either. I don't show my feelings very much: I couldn't show them in front of the children, because they didn't know for a while, and her parents didn't either. My parents felt it almost the worst because they were a long way away and my father was ill, so my mother could do nothing to help. My in-laws helped look after the children, but they were also visiting their only son who was in hospital having a heart operation: their only two children in different hospitals at the same time.

So the time was fairly full for them, but when you've got things to do it does take your mind off the grief: it doesn't become any easier, you just think about it less as such. I don't show my feelings too easily, but the children nevertheless could see that something was happening. I don't think we give children enough credit, or enough information. When I did tell them in the end, my eldest son burst into tears and cried for about ten minutes, and that was his reaction over and done with. My middle daughter, who was eight, didn't turn a hair, and the young one was too young to know anyway: they took it exceptionally well and I had no option but to react with them. I wasn't allowed to go into my shell or to show too much grief – not necessarily that it would be wrong to show it in front of them, but at first they didn't know that she was dying, although I'm sure my eldest son sensed it: we visited her every Sunday and they must have seen the deterioration.

We are religious, but not fanatics: we have always been to church with the children, and it was a positive comfort: from my wife's point of view it was something to hang on to. We had communion quite a few times in hospital, which helped us, and we did a lot of praying. I don't believe that her strength, the way she took the whole thing at the end, was man-given, it could only have been some extra force that was doing it. She was cheerful, she was the life and soul of the cancer ward, and nothing was too much trouble for her: she was absolutely remarkable. She was in pain, she must have suffered, but she never really complained. It was amazing: it even amazed our vicar. I can't imagine that I would ever be like that myself. I think to some extent life is predestined, that things are mapped out for you. God chooses the ones he wants to take and it's up to the person as to how they take it: she was able to take it very well. Believing as she did in something else gave her courage and God-given strength to cope with the situation.

I think about her from the point of view of wouldn't it be nice for her to be here to see the progress that the children are making. But there you are, it wasn't to be, so it wasn't to be. I was with her when she died, but she wasn't conscious at the end. When I was very young I saw my grandfather die, just of old age, and it had no effect on me that I can remember. I have only ever once really shown my emotions and that was when the Aberfan disaster took place: it is two miles from my home and it is the only time I have ever broken down.

Her parents are coping exceptionally well: they get to see the children a lot and we keep very closely in touch. They can help out a little around the house and they have still got the children to enjoy. Friends have been very supportive with lots of offers of help, but for the children's sake it's wrong to take up too many of them and push them all over the place. So I've kept it to three people that they stay with – my in-laws, a friend who lives down the road, and my sister-in-law. I'm basically covered: if one of them can't come or falls ill, then another one will hold the fort. That is where we needed friends and family.

I prefer to be as self-sufficient as possible: I decided that I would have to do things in the house like washing and ironing and sewing on the buttons. They are very simple things but nonetheless I am not used to doing them. I'm no cook, I am hopeless, but I decided that I must do the things on a regular basis which I might have to do in an emergency. The children are generally very good – my daughter hoovers around, and the shoes are cleaned every night. They are very good around the house, making the beds and cleaning. It's a heavy burden but the children will have clean clothes as necessary, and this friend down the road will buy clothes for the eight-year-old – my dress-sense is hopeless, I always relied on my wife to tell me what tie to wear with what shirt! It doesn't get any easier as life goes on but I have the satisfaction of knowing that I am doing most of it myself: having that inner satisfaction that you are still together as a family makes up for an awful lot. Things get me down a little bit now and again, but time is very full, particularly in the evenings when one has got to organise things: so much of it is a question of organisation. I think I can organise: it is one of my greatest abilities, I think, and I therefore feel quite confident that I should be able to sort myself round most things: I know how to do things, what to do and when to do it. It's probably very therapeutic. It makes me appreciate now what my wife did: I didn't before – men don't, until they're forced to do it for themselves.

Obviously I'd still prefer to have her around, very much so. We were very happily married for fifteen years. If I do start missing her, I think, 'That's life, that's it, it happened and there's nothing I can do to resurrect it.' She doesn't have a grave: it was one of the things we were able to talk about before she died, which again was a positive help. Because she didn't die suddenly we were able to talk about things like cremation, which she wanted, and, more important, she said, 'I don't want you spending time visiting something – a gravestone or whatever; remember me for the good things, not for the fact that I died,' which again is very positive. Even though things were very sad, her answer to me was, 'Look at it this way: in your old age you will have a family young enough to look after you.'

I have never been able to recall dreams: I have always been a person to sleep very well. One can worry, one can show concern, but because of the positive attitude we were taking I came to the frame of mind that if I didn't sleep, the children would suffer all over again. Even if I get over it now, they are the ones who are going to suffer, not me. So I was forced to say, 'Look, you have got to get the children to their schools. It's no use lying in bed moping, they've got to cope with the situation and they'll probably feel it far worse than I will.' So I make sure that they are cared for, and not passed from pillar to post, and not neglected. I was able to carry on sleeping, generally, and I took no pills – I won't take them unless I'm really ill. I had a medical checkup and everything was fine, so all being well I shan't die off too early: you never know of course. But I am the only one left now as far as the children are concerned.

I'm told that I've shown the stress and tension a bit in my work: my demand for perfection went up. Some of my subordinates had a rough time of it, largely because time was so pressing and I've had to think that much more quickly. Fortunately I never let this place get on top of me so I didn't get into a vicious circle of trouble at home and trouble at work; I've been able to cope fairly steadily with the job. I've started to get in a little bit late in the mornings, but only ten minutes, no more. I make sure that I go on time or a little bit early. I only had four days off work during the whole thing, including during the time in hospital with her, and for the funeral. Obviously there were some hours in between which I had off, but I felt able to cope and work was never a drag. I think it is important to have an outlet: I could come to work and if necessary sit here and do nothing. I can concentrate, though – if you let things go then it's much more difficult to fetch up to full steam again. I think now I have come back to full steam: it obviously has affected my work a little, but I don't think it has affected my judgement. I strive for perfection more than I did in the past and I allow less for mistakes from subordinates.

I didn't feel angry or resentful that this should happen to my family: I saw it as a thing which I could do nothing to change except by praying and try to change it that way. But if it was to be it was to be, and I convinced myself that God knew best. I don't think you have to be deeply religious, but I convinced myself that there was a purpose behind what was happening. With my wife being so positive about it, I wasn't allowed to feel angry. When I was visiting her in hospital my life was far more hectic and I was too busy to have time to think about what was happening. We have never stopped talking about her if necessary: we don't keep raising the subject but if it slips out then I say, 'Yes, wouldn't it be nice if she were here,' or whatever. They have taken it marvellously, and they are still doing quite well at school. They don't seem to be significantly affected by what has happened; obviously they are in some ways, but maybe they're very good at hiding it: or else we are doing what we have to do effectively.

I haven't really had time to feel sorry for myself. What I have is the task of sorting everything out and making sure I know where everything is. And I had to write about sixty letters after the funeral: it was nice to read all the letters that came and to know how well-loved she was. So many people did write, and it helped me in a way. There were lots of offers of help. But I didn't have time to let it sink in much: people came round and saw me, but mostly they found out from friends down the road that I had enough help with the children so most of them left me alone, which I welcomed. I had so much to do. My wife told the vicar quite straight that I wasn't to be troubled: if I wanted help I could ask for it and that since I had far more to do, my time was critical and the last thing I would want was people coming and having a chat about it. When people came around I obviously didn't kick them out but it was kept to a reasonable level: I couldn't have stood, time-wise, a lot of people coming round. In any case I am not the kind of person who can easily talk about things in general, and I don't need someone to talk to about what happened. I don't know how I would feel if I didn't have anything to do: possibly I would have too much time to spend thinking about it. I would need something to keep my mind off it, and then perhaps talking about it would help. If I kept sitting down and thinking about it I'd let myself go to rack and ruin.

I'm forced to look ahead but that doesn't frighten me. I

take solace from the fact that I can't see that what has happened now is going to change. I'll take the future as it comes, I don't fear the future at all, only in that I must live: I've got to live to look after the children. I'm the only one that they've got now, and that concerns me. I think the future has a lot going for it. Children always give you problems but nevertheless they are always different: I am only concerned that I can cope with the demands of the children on top of work and everything else. I won't know until the situations themselves arise: I shall therefore assume that I can cope with anything that crops up.

Obviously there is an emotional gap: I would remarry if the right person came along. My wife plainly told me to. She said, 'If you can find a nice widow, you get yourself married.' Although I feel that marriage is for life, there are circumstances that ordain it not to be so. My wife's gone, but she said, 'You remarry, for the children's sake if nothing else. Whereas you've got a shorter time to live, they've got a nice long life ahead of them.'

I don't feel I can leave the children at weekends to have time to myself: there is so much to do for them and anyway there's just that little impetus which I need behind me, which I haven't got now, that I used to have. On occasions I have to force myself to do the jobs that she used to do. I can't really relax totally now: I think about a holiday but I'm not sure that a week on my own would benefit me that much. I'm not sure either how I would fare if I took a week off when the children are off school: I don't think I could do it, cooking for them every lunchtime, because my cooking is so basic – cheese on toast and beans on toast! I couldn't commit myself to a casserole, not quite yet. I will: I am determined to later on.

I am exhausted by the time I get to bed at night: I find I like my bed. I have always preferred to get up early and go to bed early. The exhaustion doesn't really carry through – I feel tired I suppose, but there again if you have got to get up in the morning, you don't worry about it, you forget about what you feel. I've got to get to work and I've got to get the children to school. At the weekends we used to have a lie-in and the children still have a cup of tea in bed with me on

Saturdays and Sundays. I think that's important because we always used to.

There are times in between all this action, I have to admit, when I do feel wouldn't it be nice if she was here to help out when things get a bit on top of me. But when she was in hospital I was forced to think, 'Nobody is going to get me out of this so I might as well get out of it myself.' I can't help missing her, but things are becoming routine – it's four months now and already the children are beginning to do some spadework for me in the way of suggesting outings and so on. Life is so varied day by day with the various things that happen.

I convinced myself that she is up there waiting for us to join her and that therefore perhaps she can see what I'm up to: so I've got to behave myself – in the nicest sort of way, not in an oppressive way. I'm quite happy to think that she is up there, seeing us and watching down, looking after us. I suppose it gives me a bit of comfort to think that – making sure I don't fall off into the deep end. But it wouldn't inhibit me from remarrying: I would still expect the children to recognise her as their mother, and the person I married would have to accept that point of view.

There have been some very interesting practical problems surrounding the business of death. I could answer all the questions from the bank about probate quite happily, but when I went to register the death I filled the forms in and then I was given another form to take off to the Department of Social Security to collect the death grant. I had to sit around waiting and then they gave me another one, a four-page form, to fill in. Why on earth couldn't they have given them all to me at once? I had to have all the National Insurance numbers and birth certificates and marriage certificate and I had to go home again to fill it all in. I couldn't make some of it out: you are never quite sure what these forms mean. It's no wonder that some of the older people get flummoxed. I think they could make it a lot easier by saying, 'Here is a set of forms which might apply to you – they are hard reading but they will give you most of the things that you need.' They have an ideal opportunity when someone goes to register a death: give them a little packet of all the forms saying what things are and what claims you can make. Nobody told me about the child benefit allowance, for example – I stumbled across that one by accident: and I may say I am still waiting for the books to come through.

The other thing that some people don't realise is the question of bank accounts: we made sure we had a joint account because then you just carry on as normal. If it's a personal bank account, however, it is frozen when the person dies. A joint account comes by survivorship, like my house – my wife didn't need to make a will to cover it because it was in joint ownership. So it meant that I could go on spending money, but if the account had been frozen I would have been stuck for money, which with three children to look after isn't funny. There are all the fees for death certificates, under-takers, cremation – they won't cremate until you have paid the fees. People don't seem to know about these things; I suppose they don't talk about them because they have a fear of death. They won't discuss it, but I do think that certain things should be stressed to people. I told the undertaker about my idea for simplifying the form-filling, and he said, 'You just try and get past the Civil Service!' But it would make such a difference to older people: they can't run around these places: it's bad enough finding out where the nearest social security office is.

I wasn't too sure what I would do with her ashes; I didn't know whether to send them to the church or not in the casket. I decided in the end not to: I couldn't quite see the point, so I rang the vicar after the cremation and asked him to arrange for them to be scattered. He just told me to ring the crematorium myself: I was disgusted. It was so clinical of him, and he's up there every day as it is. He could have made that call for me in the circumstances. Anyway, in the end I had the ashes scattered over the crematorium garden, on consecrated ground, two days later. I was back at work by then and I asked them to do it for me. I often worry whether I should have done something and been there, but I made the decision then, and that's life. There are a few questions that one could re-raise, but what's the point in doing that? You can't do anything about it; you can't put the clock back. Otherwise our vicar was exceptionally good.

By agreement with my wife I never stayed there overnight, even when she was unconscious. There was an incident in the hospital when a woman there was dying in the cancer ward and her husband was there beside her for three days and three nights. He left to go downstairs for a cup of tea and she died. My wife said, 'Don't you do that for me. What's the point? You can't do a thing, it's pointless.' The two nights before the end our vicar went there and spent half the night at her bedside, which helped her. It was very good of him. The staff at the hospital were very good, I couldn't fault them: they were open with me, kind to the children, and the nurses who were on the cancer ward really knew how to deal with people. Those nurses are grossly underpaid, particularly those who specialise in those sort of cases. It is very demanding and they deserve far more than they get. They suffer because of their own dedication.

I got all her clothes together and put them in one wardrobe. The hats I have given away, and my daughter has got all the handkerchiefs. The rest of the clothes are still there: I'll wait to see what happens – they are too good to be given away but if I find the right opportunity I'll do whatever I think is right with them. It doesn't worry me to have them there, and I prefer to sort them out myself. I didn't want anyone to come around and sort my wife's things out; I'll do it in my own time so that I know where everything is. Some things might suit my daughter when she grows up, and I might find somebody in a couple of years who might be the same size as my wife. If not, then they can go. It's not as if scarves and gloves are that special to people. Time will tell.

When she died I came home on the train: my father-in-law wanted to come and pick me up but I said, 'I'll come home on the train.' At that particular time isolation was the right thing for me, and not to have people around who knew what had happened. I preferred to come home on my own and let myself come to grips with it, and settle myself down and let it sink in. After that it was down to work: things do work out alright in the end.

14

JANE:
her husband

Jane is forty-one and has moved to a quiet street in South London since her husband, Henry, died of a heart attack three years ago. He was forty when he died and had a career in the army. She was left with their three children who are now seventeen, fourteen and eleven. She and Henry had been happily married for fifteen years and had travelled around a great deal, moving house almost every year. After his death she had to find, with some difficulty, a new home for herself and the children, and is now trying to adjust to a very different way of life.

Parting is all we know of heaven
And all we need of hell.

Emily Dickinson

Henry died very suddenly, but he had been unwell for three months; we couldn't understand what was causing it. So although it wasn't a bolt from the blue, one is never prepared for it. They could find nothing wrong when they had done all the tests and it didn't occur to us that anything could happen. The hospital said, 'This is very good news, come back in another week and we'll do more tests.' In the week he was out of hospital he fell down dead.

In the first five minutes my initial reaction was disbelief, and yet total acceptance at the same time. I knew what had happened before I got there. My youngest son, unfortunately, was with him. It was a Sunday morning and I was having a bath. Henry had pills that he had to take if he felt a pain coming on and he was out in the garden loading stuff on to the top of the car, which he shouldn't have been doing. He obviously felt a pain because he turned to Julian and said, 'Go and get my pills from the front of the car.' Julian came rushing up and shouted, 'Come quickly, Daddy's fainted.' I knew before I got out of the bath what had happened: I went down, took one look and I knew what had happened. At the same time I couldn't believe it because he was still warm. I kept thinking, 'He's still warm so he must be all right.' I couldn't think what to do next and a few seconds later – it seemed like half an hour – I rang the doctor. After that there was an extraordinary feeling of complete calm. We were supposed to be going out to lunch and my parents were also supposed to be going. The doctor said, 'Can you get hold of someone to come and be with you?' and I remember picking up the phone and saying quite calmly to Daddy, 'I'm so glad I caught you. Can you get here on the way because Henry is dead.' Looking back on it it must have sounded extraordinary to be so cool and calm: it was a shock reaction which numbed the system totally.

The numbness lasted, in retrospect, far too long: that evening a realisation started to dawn a little bit, but only just. The only time I cried that day was very briefly when my parents arrived. The thing that made me cry then was the children, because the two older ones were away at school and what hit me was that they were going to have to be told and they were away from home. I remember saying to my father, 'Those poor children,' but it didn't occur to me to cry for myself. It just hadn't sunk in. Julian had screamed with fright when he first realised what had happened and then he went completely calm and started playing with his toys.

When we had made all the dreadful initial arrangements my parents said, 'Right, we'll take you back with us,' because we had only been back in our house six days and there was almost nothing in it. When we got home my parents were quite unable to help, they were so stunned themselves. I couldn't blame them, but we sat in almost uncomfortable silence, nobody knowing what to say next. I can't really remember what happened. I did go to bed but still couldn't cry; I was like a caged lion. I kept standing up and sitting down and then walking around and I thought I was a bit peculiar. I have discovered since that this is quite normal and it can go on for some time. I remember getting up in the middle of the night and walking round the room and then trying to get back into bed to go back to sleep again, and then having to get up again. I don't think anyone thought of such a thing as a sleeping tablet and I'd certainly never taken one in my life before so I didn't have any with me. Funnily enough the insomnia only lasted two or three days, until after the funeral. Until then I was wound up like a clock. After that I slept extremely well for quite a long time, and then I started to get bad nights about six months later.

Funnily enough I didn't dream about Henry at all during that six months until a very close friend, who was one of the few people who talked to me and to whom I could talk, said, 'Do you dream about Henry?' I said, 'It is the most extraordinary thing, but I never have.' From that night on I started to dream about him; she unlocked something. I had a rather distressing dream; first of all I dreamt that it had happened and then I dreamt that it hadn't and I woke up thinking it was all right. All sorts of dreams like he came back and what I said when he came back. It was distressing, the dreaming, but once I'd dreamt all those dreams I stopped dreaming about him again. Occasionally now I dream that he's come back: it's very upsetting because it comes as a bolt from the blue – I expected it at the time, but not now.

I found the funeral much easier than I thought. My doctor gave me a tranquillizer, which had a magical effect and I was quite calm. Everything that happened I remember exactly; in a curious way I almost enjoyed it – it sounds a terrible thing to say. But I felt he was still there. All our friends were there and a lot of people came along for tea afterwards. I was pleased to see them and I felt, 'There's no point in being unable to talk to anyone, I must go and talk to all these people. They've come a long way, isn't it fun to see them.' I did find it very difficult at one moment and that was when they actually took the body out. That was the difficult part because there was a finality about it then. They cremated him and I didn't go to that because none of the family did: he had a military funeral and was taken off by the military people – that's the way he would have liked it. I thought it was too much for all of us and it wasn't really what I wanted to do. So my parting was at the funeral. It was beautiful. It was a lovely service and in a funny way it wasn't sad. It was when we got home afterwards that there was this terrible feeling of anti-climax and suddenly the restlessness came back all over again. I think that nature gives you a boost of some kind: the tension is so great that it amounts to a form of excitement which carries you along; once the tension stops you haven't got enough energy left to keep it going, and then comes a depression.

The restlessness lasted about a fortnight and then I got flu and had to go to bed: it was the best thing that could have happened because I climbed into bed and wept for four days without stopping. I was all by myself in the house and I didn't want anyone around, I wanted to be by myself. It was a very good thing, I unbottled that initial part a little bit. Then I started to write letters, which in itself is a very good way of letting go because it's so emotional getting them and then writing back. The letters helped me enormously – there were one or two very special ones, and I still read them, they are still helpful. It helps to know that other people are as or almost as sad as you are; which, of course, they are. One tends to think you're the only one who feels it, but of course it's not so. There are an awful lot of people who feel it, and this helps to keep a sense of proportion.

After that it was a question of getting on with life a little bit and getting through each day. I found it impossibly difficult to think ahead; so long as I was doing something on Monday and getting through it, that was OK. I forgot things totally. Shopping was a physical impossibility – it would take me hours to do a normal day's shopping: I would stand in the supermarket and not even know what I was doing there. I thought I was cracking up: I couldn't concentrate and I had an extraordinary fear of having to leave the house at one moment, then not wanting to be out and having to rush back to the security of home; and then feeling almost trapped by the house and wanting to get out again. Tremendous swings of irrational feelings: one minute one thing and the next completely the opposite. The conflict and confusion of feelings was frightening. It worried me: being a reasonably balanced, normal person, suddenly to have this inability to manage one's own emotions at all was very strange.

I felt very tired – exhausted and drained: I still do. One of the things I've learned is that when I feel a crunch coming I now let it happen, whereas before I used to fight it and try to keep on going. I would sleep and not wake up at all refreshed. Waking up is the worst part of the day: there's a sudden realisation because there's an instant when you have forgotten, and when you wake up it all comes flooding back and you think, 'Shall I get out of bed or shan't I?' I found there were two sorts of crying – sometimes it doesn't help at all and sometimes it does: it's like having surface tears and deep-down tears. Surface tears don't really help, but if you can get almost hysterical, it releases something. It's almost like having a tummy bug and if you can be sick you feel better. It's literally poisoning your system the longer you hold it in.

I was very, very hypersensitive, and irritable. I was also quite unable to predict how I would react in given circumstances and I still find this to a certain extent. Suddenly things would upset me that wouldn't have done yesterday and probably wouldn't again tomorrow: mundane everyday things. The children were a help and a comfort, but at times I was very short with them. William was thirteen and almost adult enough to understand a little bit. Julian was eight, and a complete child. I did worry about him. He's better now, but he wouldn't let me out of his sight, he was terrified, having seen his father die in front of him. If I sat in a chair and closed my eyes he'd come rushing up and shake me and say, 'Mummy, are you all right?' and I would realise that he was thinking I'd done the same. I could understand it totally but I found it very irritating because I wanted to be by myself. I encouraged him to talk about it and made him go through it time and time again exactly what had happened because, rightly or wrongly, I felt it was a good thing. We still talk about him a lot, it's not a taboo subject. It comes quite naturally.

Later on I began to feel angry that this should happen to me; but not initially. Initially I astonished myself by being so calm and accepting it all, I was convinced that it was the right thing for him, for it to have happened like that because it would have been disastrous for him to have been an invalid. He'd been active mentally and physically, he'd played a lot of games and been very capable: he'd have been miserable. I kept saying to myself, 'This is a good thing, it was so quick, he couldn't have known anything, how marvellous, and if it had to happen thank God it was this way.' There were certain times I thought, 'Why did he have to go and leave me; I can't shut the garage door,' and, 'Why aren't you here to fix this or that?' Silly little things. But later on I started to feel guilty. I thought that it was my fault and that I was being punished for having been a scratchy wife. I felt it very strongly. I'm told by people I talk to or things I have read, that this is quite common but I didn't realise it at the time and again I thought I was going dotty. It would have helped me if I'd known about it at the time: if you are expecting a baby you buy a book and you want to find out 'Should I be feeling this or that?' There are so many strong feelings in grief, strong emotions, that you wonder whether you should be feeling like that.

Sometimes when the telephone rang I used to rush to it thinking he was ringing me up; and I would rush to the door when the mail came. Sometimes in the early days I heard the door slam and think he would be walking in. It was so very real, almost to the point of hallucination. It was a horrid shock each time, but that is something that passes, because you get accustomed to a different way of life and when somebody hasn't come in and slammed the door for a year you don't expect it any more. There were terrible feelings of remorse, of regret about things I had or hadn't done. Obviously everybody has ups and downs but ours was basically a very good marriage: I think in a moment of depression you hang on to the negative things and blow them up out of all proportion until the whole thing becomes distorted. There is an awful lot of anger involved too, which one doesn't realise until later and you need something to trigger off a catharsis of letting out anger. You need to get it out of your system – I shouted and ranted and raved and screamed, but not until quite recently; much too late, really. Sometimes I take it out on others, but mostly I do it to myself. Physical activity helps that – like digging the garden.

My social life changed of course although there were variations on a theme. Some people asked me out initially because they felt they must; they'd do it once or twice and then they'd fade out. The hardcore friends always did ask me and there was never anyone to make up the numbers. There were some who didn't invite me because I was an inconvenient guest. No doubt some of it is imagined but you do feel that you're being cast out a little bit. People want to feel that they've done their bit, and then they can switch off. They mostly don't know what to say: there are certain people who feel much more comfortable if you are being normal and your old self. This is the danger, because you then tend to behave normally because you feel this is expected of you: you try to be bright and cheerful and it isn't a good thing, it puts even more stress on you. You become quite an accomplished actor and eventually you have to stop doing that: I certainly went on doing it for far too long. I realise now, three years later, that I was cracking up: I reached the point where I didn't think I was ever, ever going to get better, and a lot of it was that I was trying to keep going and be strong. So I went to a counsellor and she made me realise that I must stop behaving the way I felt I ought to and just get on and be. She outlined some of the symptoms I was suffering that I didn't recognise as symptoms.

One of the reasons it took me so long was that there was a year in the middle when I had to move house and find a new home: I was in suspended animation, completely in a vacuum. Everything stood still for that year – we weren't progressing with life, we were searching for a house, and so one whole year was taken away from the process of healing.

When we finally got into the house I went, 'Phew! We've got a roof over our heads,' and it was then that it suddenly hit me: we were on our own, there was nothing familiar anymore, and nobody to do the new home with. I overestimated my own abilities: having moved house fifteen times in fifteen years I thought I could manage, but of course it was so different on my own. Yet I don't find practical things so difficult because Henry was away such a lot: once we had to spend a year apart and in some ways this is why it took me so long to come to terms with the fact that he wasn't coming back – I still felt I was ticking off the days on a calendar rather like a child does. It was the emotional loneliness that was so difficult, and the lack of sharing. Making a decision without him to refer to was almost impossible, and this was one of the things that worried me. I got to the point where I couldn't decide whether we'd have mince or liver for lunch: I had taken so many decisions moving house that suddenly the system stopped.

I think not being able to share the happy things is more difficult than not being able to share the practical difficulties like the broken garage door. When there has been a good or happy thing or a good day or we've all had a happy time, then there is no one to share it with and that is what is more difficult. It's something that people don't altogether understand; you can become very silent in the middle of a lovely party and everyone thinks you're very peculiar. They can't understand that it's because it suddenly hits you, the loneliness in the middle of something good. It's something you don't understand unless you've experienced it for yourself. The loneliness varies: it depends on what the day has been like – it's not always the evenings that are bad. Sometimes the mornings are the worst. It's that business of getting up and started, because when there are no children in the house and they are all away at school, there isn't the incentive to leap up and get going. There's no human contact which in itself is generative. It requires a lot of self-discipline to live alone successfully, there's no doubt about that, but you must achieve it in order to go forward. You've got to make yourself because the children depend on it.

I've got lots of friends dotted about, and I am starting to make new friends. I wouldn't say I have a particularly active social life; it's no good pretending that suddenly you are back to being young and gay, I'm not. In some ways I don't know that that is what I really want: it's running away from it if you want to be dashing about every night, and that's not what I want. One must learn to be able to sit with oneself, which is what is so difficult to learn to do. Especially if you are, like me, the last of the great uneducated. We weren't ever taught anything, I did a secretarial course and then was told to find a gentleman and marry. People who have careers, the next generation, are better off in some ways. They've got an education to fall back on.

I see less of my parents now – I am their only child and they've tried their very best to help but in some ways I have pushed them away and almost refused to accept help from them, partly because I was determined to get through by myself. They wanted me to go back and I did go home for a while: it was a disaster, they thought I was back to being their little girl again and this was not constructively helpful at all. I almost had to do a kind of breakaway. Perhaps I made it more difficult for myself by not turning to them.

Initially I was totally unable to eat for about a week, otherwise my grief didn't manifest itself in physical ways: except that there was a feeling inside of pain – emotional pain can be almost physical. It's almost impossible to describe but it's something like being all out of place inside, torn, as if you've been gouged out. I did eventually get some sleeping tablets simply because I thought if I didn't get a good night's sleep I would end up totally exhausted. I didn't take any tranquillizers at all. I am anti-pills basically and I don't really like taking sleeping pills. I'm much more likely to rush for a drink, which is all right if you do it in moderation, but in fact it is extremely depressing if you drink too much. It's not a good thing, but it's very easy to do.

Occasionally I do feel sorry for myself, I have to admit. I think this should never have been done to me because I am not able to deal with it. I'm not able to cope with it, I'm not the sort of person who should have been left; masses of other people can cope, but I can't. When I feel that I'm achieving nothing and getting nowhere, I endeavour not to show it because I don't think it helps. Self-pity certainly doesn't win you friends. This was where the counsellor was helpful because she made me sit down and list the things I have achieved, however small: 'Tell yourself, could you have done this when your husband was alive?' and it was astonishing how many things you have achieved which you probably couldn't have done before. It was very good therapy.

It's so difficult to know whether you are getting it right with the children: one of the most difficult things is trying to be a loving mother and a disciplinarian father at the same time. You can get it terribly wrong by being too tough or not tough enough. It's a very real difficulty, particularly when your energy is at a low ebb anyway. You need support.

Religion did help me – I've always been not exactly religious, but I've felt that there is something there, certainly. Henry was a very devout Catholic, but a very human one and not at all bigoted. He had a very strong faith and I used to wonder what it was he had got and was slightly envious because I hadn't got it. I later discovered a little bit perhaps of what he had got in a funny sort of way. I think there is no doubt about it, you are helped somehow; there is something there that I do believe in. I go to church and I very often believe that my prayers are answered, maybe not in the way that I am expecting – very often they are not – but nevertheless something usually crops up. Without any doubt Henry is, in a sense, somewhere: that I do believe. There are moments when if there is something difficult that I've got to deal with, I literally talk to him and say, 'Now, come on, you've got to be with me on this occasion,' and I'm certain that something gets through. It's lovely. It doesn't always work for more trivial things, but he's definitely still watching when I need him but not when I don't. He's not around all the time, but he is occasionally, when I need him.

My mother-in-law took it very hard. He was her only son and she doesn't get on particularly well with her other child, her daughter, and she doted on him, so she took it very badly. Yet if anything our relationship has improved: I used to find her difficult because she was very possessive towards him and resented me, like many mothers-in-law. But now we get on extremely well. That's something good that's come out of it; there are obviously a lot of good things. I suppose my relationship with the children is closer, certainly with my daughter: we both found her difficult and in a funny way I have got closer to her as a result of him not being there, which is a cruel thing to say. I've been forced to look at the situation and adapt, and try and make it better, to try and use the strength that I have got. Undoubtedly from a personal point of view it has given me a far greater depth of understanding and compassion, and a sense of perception – seeing what I might never have noticed before in other people: whether they are suffering or whether they are showing me a kindness, either way. Certainly it's made me stop and notice and see, and that is a very good thing. One does gain a certain something from having been through pain and emotional suffering: it isn't all bad.

Talking about it helped me at the time: I wanted to talk endlessly. I became completely possessed by the fact that I wanted to talk: I wanted to go over it again and again. Very few people would understand this and listen and not think, 'Oh dear she's talking about it again.' They are the ones who help, people who will come up and ask you straight, 'How do you feel about it all? Do you still feel this and that? Do you think you might get married again?' Obviously they are questions that are uppermost in your mind, but a lot of people are terrified of asking. They are longing to know the answer, but they're frightened to ask. Provided they ask you in a sensitive way or a natural way, it isn't in the least offensive and nor is any other question. After all, one hasn't become someone from a different planet suddenly.

If you compare it to an operation, when you have a physical injury you are bandaged up and have medical treatment for as long as you need it. People understand that you are an invalid and that you need to be treated accordingly. If you have a major spiritual or emotional injury, the same needs apply – or even greater needs since there are very few effective aids that can help effect the cure. Because nobody can actually see with their own eyes the injury, they treat you as if you were normal and healthy, which you are not: you need to be treated as some kind of an invalid at a time when you are least capable of looking after yourself.

I had three or four friends who were an immense help, and one or two people I didn't know very well were strangely enough a great help just briefly. They came out with things and asked questions and allowed me to talk without being worried as to how they would react. A lot of the time I was exhausted because I was carrying other people's feelings as well: I would often be the one that was trying to keep the conversation going or to cover up because they felt they'd said something wrong. It is tiring, it's not the way round it should be, but you can't blame people.

Music helped me particularly, I'm very fond of music; it has the same effect as valium or a whisky. If I feel wound up I listen to some music, and poetry helps to a certain extent. I think things come into sharper focus suddenly: perhaps you could call it an increased reverence for life – the beautiful cherry blossom you perhaps might not ever have noticed you suddenly think is gorgeous and you actually stop and look at it. I love gardening and I find it very therapeutic: it covers every aspect because if you feel you need to let out anger you can dig or cut something down; if you are feeling creative you can plant or tend, or you can sit and look if you feel exhausted.

As far as ritual goes, Henry was cremated, which is something we had in fact discussed and I knew that was all right. But I don't believe in pushing the harrowing bit too far; the fact that we had what amounted to a party afterwards was a good thing – that part of a wake is essentially happy. I'm not sure that the harrowing bit achieves anything – would the person want you to be sitting there in a sodden heap? I don't think they would. One of the things that carried me through practically everything was that Henry would want me to be doing this and that and not the other. I think people sending flowers is nice: it's lovely to get them, and I think letters are nice too: they helped me. There was one person who rang me that same night she'd heard and that was marvellous, because

I felt there was one person who dared to ring up and talk normally.

There's a Book of Remembrance at the crematorium and there is a leaf in it for him, but I've never been there, I don't feel a need to. There was a moment when I suddenly wished that I had gone to the cremation, and wished a lot of things: but I don't feel a need now. I went back to a lot of regimental functions as a way of almost going back, almost to gouge it a little deeper. It's a sort of masochism that makes one go and do things which are going to be difficult, in order to get over it.

I've still got all his clothes, partly because I've got two sons and I thought I must never get rid of anything that might do for them. I got rid of his army uniform on the first day: I couldn't bear to have it in the house, because it reminded me of his death. I blamed work and his job for killing him, which it didn't, but it was a way of laying the blame and I thought I must get it all out of the way. All the rest of his things are around and William uses them: it doesn't worry me, I rather like it. I don't know whether it's a good thing or not.

The stage we've reached now is one of acceptance, final acceptance that he is not going to come back and it is never going to be as it was. That has finally sunk in. It's almost the most difficult stage because you're not battling any more with getting over something, there's a kind of endless vacuum. It's very difficult to look forward because you wonder what to look at. There's a void in front and what is there to look forward for? or to? You have to create little things to look forward to. I still can't look far ahead; I daren't let myself think about five years' time because I think, 'Oh God, how am I going to get through five years?' Ultimately I probably want to get married again, but I don't at this moment. I thought I did but I don't think I'm ready to. I've become so nearly self-sufficient now that I feel I must get it complete. There is a terrible danger if I got married again now of going straight back to being totally reliant again on the other person and that would be an awful mistake: I don't know how long I need but there's another step to be taken so that I am a whole person in myself before I take on another person. Because

the second time round is so very different to the first: you're
not going to have any children, your own children are
growing away from you, you are going to be alone with that
person for the rest of your days and that is a very different
situation. It requires a great deal more thought if you are
going to be happy and I'm not quite sure enough of myself.

But it's unnatural living alone; apart from anything else
it's so much more fun to have somebody else to communicate
with. It's not so much the fear of loneliness or old age, it's just
that life is endlessly more fun with two sharing. There's lots to
be had out of life without being married but it's more of a
struggle when there's no give and take and no support. There
is a loneliness in carrying responsibilities alone, and every
now and then it's overwhelming.

I do find anniversaries difficult; I try not to say that a
certain date is going to be worse than any other because the
middle of the summer can be just as bad as the middle of
February, which is when he died, but it's almost a subcon-
scious thing. I'll have a migraine the week before – and when
the day comes it's a kind of death. I suppose it's worse
because you tend to relive it: it's just more concentrated than
other days. I find that Christmas and Easter are almost more
difficult to get through because they are not just one day,
they are chunks of days, and we would have been doing
things together. And there are occasions like for instance
when the children first come back for the school holidays –
that's a day I find particularly difficult because suddenly they
are back, there is noise everywhere, dirty clothes flying in all
directions and everyone's telling me all at once what they've
been doing and then they go off upstairs and suddenly I'm
sitting there alone and I think, 'This is the moment when
Henry would have been saying, "Hasn't William changed?"'
Again it's something that people don't appreciate, they say,
'You must be looking forward to the holidays,' and of course
you are; but you know what is going to happen.

Eventually the reactions become predictable and you can
try and teach yourself to sway the other way. It does after a
bit get better: one of the most helpful letters I had was from a
sweet aunt, herself a widow, who said, 'It will get better

simply because no human could tolerate the degree of pain as it is at this moment, forever. Therefore you have to believe that it will get better.' It was a very good thing to have written because it doesn't go away but it does get better: it changes and becomes less searingly painful, but more of a dull ache. Yet it can come back very suddenly without any warning at all: it'll just pierce me and then it's worse than it was at the beginning because I was with it all the time at the beginning; but now it hits me out of the blue and I am unprepared for the pain.

15

GILES:
his wife

*Giles was thirty-four when, four months ago, his wife Cathy
drowned accidentally in the pond in their garden during heavy
winter snow. In spite of valiant attempts to rescue her from
under the ice he was unable to do so. She was thirty-three and
they had two adopted sons, Paul and Edward, aged five and
four. Suddenly, overnight, Giles was faced with having to
continue his job as an executive of a local factory, to care for
his children, and at the same time cope with the shock and
adjust to the loneliness of being a widower. He was helped by
the presence of a close and loving family: his parents and
brother, who live nearby, were able to offer much support. He
employed a nanny to look after the children. This was his
second experience of close bereavement, and indeed of sudden
accidental death in the family: eleven years ago his sister, aged
twenty-one, of whom he was very fond, was killed with her
husband in a car crash on the continent.*

**Pain is a holy angel who shows treasure to man which
otherwise remains forever hidden.**

Adalbert Stifler

I was extremely fond of my sister. We grew up together and
did an awful lot with each other. We were fairly close in age
and we got on very well. She was younger and therefore,
being a girl, she was socially at much the same stage as I was.
We went to the same places and did the same things, tore

around in the same crazy cars and all the stupid things you do in your teens and early twenties. When she was nineteen she got married to a guy who was great fun.

I don't think any of the family ever expressed any resentment towards the lorry driver who killed them. We had no sense of anger; in fact we all felt extremely sorry for him. He'd done something we could all have done in our time: he had driven up from the south of France through the night, and at about six a.m. he fell asleep at the wheel. We've all driven home from a party tight, we've all done stupid things in cars, but just because we haven't killed anybody it doesn't make it right. We're probably doubly stupid because we're getting away with it and the more we do it the more likely we are to end up killing somebody. Both she and my brother-in-law were asleep in the back when the car crashed so they didn't know a thing. The driver survived but his wife was killed too.

I missed her chatter and her laughter. It didn't really sink in for months. I remember walking down a street in London and running into a business friend whom I hadn't seen for nine months or so. He said, 'Hi, how are you? How's that gorgeous sister of yours?' It was like being slugged across the back of the neck. It taught me a lot actually: it was almost worse for him than it was for me. But it did open the wound.

Father had to go out to France to do the identification of my sister – as indeed he did the identification on Cathy. He didn't have to, but he did. When he got back from France he walked around the garden with me and told me the mechanics of what had happened. She was only twenty-one. From the reports we had, and from the police photographs, we could tell that it must have been instant: they wouldn't have known anything about it, which helps. The same applies to what happened here, in a way. I was there and I saw what happened to Cathy. The conditions were such that, going into that kind of icy water, it's like a club blow: you take one gasp and that's it, you're unconscious. The shock of the cold knocks you out.

If I hadn't been there and seen what happened, it would have been much worse; I would have imagined a struggle. Afterwards I felt terribly guilty that I had not been able to get her out, although I tried to desperately. They say I nearly killed myself doing it. You think you can cope with situations, you believe you can deal with whatever life chucks at you, and deal successfully: basically I live in a very successful environment, and it is by getting it right nine times out of ten, not by getting it wrong ten times out of nine. You feel a bit of an idiot: there was a perfectly simple task and I got it wrong; or else it was beyond my capability. But there's a hell of a feeling of guilt inside; at least there was until after the inquest was over. Yet I acted and reacted on instinct. Afterwards I thought, 'If only I'd remembered that; if only I'd done such and such; or I should have done that.' But it was too late. If I had been able to think rationally, I might have done things in a different way with a different result. My initial feeling was that instinct is the strongest reaction of all, but now I don't feel that.

I suppose I was shocked for a while, but in spite of seeming unreal it was in fact very real, because I'd seen it happen. Whether it was right or wrong I don't know, but I got my brother to take me over to the hospital the next day to see Cathy again. It was the time of the NUPE strikes and they hadn't cleaned her up. Yet in some ways it was a beautiful sight: she looked so completely peaceful. One half of me says that was the right thing to do, the other half says it was stupid. It would have been far better to remember her as she was. Literally a minute beforehand we'd been kicking snow at each other and laughing. I don't think that seeing her body made it quicker for me to accept that it was real: I knew it had happened, because I'd been there.

For a while instinct takes over again: you've got so much to do. That's therapy in itself. They say that funeral rites are there for a good purpose, and they do block your mind to anything for the period of time that you're so bloody busy. All those rituals are a link with the person, too, and perhaps an important bridge over the first part of loss. I made one very bad mistake: it was my choice to have Cathy's cremation in the morning at ten, and the memorial service at two thirty in the afternoon. The gap was dreadful: if you're bracing yourself for one thing you'd best brace yourself for two. After the morning you come off the top a bit and then you've got to stiffen yourself for the next one. It was entirely my fault. We didn't have a funeral lunch, which might have helped, because her parents wanted to go off on their own with my brother-in-law.

It's four months now and still to some extent I'm not back to normal physically. My appetite isn't what it was and I don't sleep all that well. I find I plan things for the day and if I get tripped up on them I get decidedly ruffled and uptight with the people around me who are preventing me from doing what I set out to do. I suppose that's how I react to the circumstances because I am so bloody busy. It was a help to be busy to start with, but it is no longer: sometimes I sit down and think, 'My God, I'm going to be worn to a frazzle if it goes on like this.' I am tense and restless, and I forget things unless I write them down; or I can beat it by putting the bucket in the middle of the hall so I know damn well I shall fall over it. It's true to say that I'm pretty irritable because I feel so exhausted most of the time.

The restlessness is a help, in a way: in general, if you take the whole aspect of living and running a house, keeping the garden going, I'm doing a hell of a lot more. I do find I can become completely absorbed at work though. There are times when I get a set of figures to work on in the factory and I can get lost in them. Very often you're working to a time and a date and you know the pressure's on and on that score there's a fear of failure; so you concentrate, and everything else goes away.

I suppose I have used alcohol to help; I have reacted by going out to parties, and one can get tight on comparatively little booze. Afterwards if I was inclined I'd wind my way through the best part of a bottle of scotch, but it just wouldn't touch the sides: I mean it wouldn't solve anything. I'd just feel like death in the morning. It's not an answer; perhaps there aren't any, yet in a way there may be. It's not an answer exactly, but I'm beginning to have an understanding of what has happened. I have been brought up and schooled in a fairly strong Christian atmosphere and when I can make myself think positively I think, 'Well, she's clearly far better off than

I am. She's gone to a far better place.' If you believe that, then it is a help, but you certainly don't believe it all the time; or it doesn't help all the time. Sometimes I feel hammered by fate. It makes me feel bewildered. I don't feel angry at fate, I've just got this numb ache and a feeling of bewilderment. At first I used to talk to myself to try and organise my brain. I used to talk to Cathy, too. I asked her things knowing no answer would come. The worst thing is getting home after parties; then the loneliness is really driven home. I feel weary and exhausted, I have to push myself all the time.

Sometimes I wonder what will happen next, not that it frightens me. But certainly I am giving considerable thought to making sure my will is clear. I'm out on the highways and byways a lot, and never a month goes by unless I pass a hell of a smash, and the next one could be mine. I still don't know where I stand legally: the lawyers and accountants are trying to work it out now: it does take a long while to sort out. I feel that the legal system is so slow: I found that an irritation, that I couldn't walk in and say, 'Right, what's the answer?' 'Well, it might be this or it might be that . . .' They are a monopoly, these lawyers, and you can't get probate without one. It's not difficult to imagine why they take their time.

I don't dream about Cathy much – I never did; or very, very rarely. I remember the good bits: like any marriage, there were good times and bad and I remember the good, in fact. We had done so much together. I have almost more a feeling of disappointment than one of regret. We worked on the house here night after night, weekend after weekend, together. We built it all ourselves. I just feel disappointed that she's not here to enjoy what she's done. I don't feel cheated, somehow, but disappointed. It's terribly lonely without her. Yet I don't feel jealous of other people who are still married; it's just a question now of how I'm going to deal with the situation.

To start with my boss was very understanding; he was fine. He gave all the indications of being a great help. 'You can stay away, or take a holiday' – which was the last thing I wanted to do: even now the idea of a holiday is awful. But he wasn't to understand that. To start with he was very good, but when, a few weeks later, he found me at my desk in tears – I just broke down and cried and cried – he said, 'Look, this isn't good enough, there's a job to be done.' Just because, from his point of view, he had thought, 'OK, that's the problem dealt with, he's back on the track again.' But as soon as I tripped up he was down on me like a ton of bricks.

There's no doubt that the experience has made me far more aware of what I see, what I touch, what I sense. It's bound to. Because it's brought home to you in glorious technicolour that life if very short and you'd best make the most of it while you're here and you'd best see it in all its colour and all its touch and all its sense. Life is very short. It's a horribly mathematical way of looking at life, but it is seventy years long: perhaps to some people it's a terrible shock if they don't get their threescore years and ten. But how many weeks is it? You can work that out in your head. Before this happened I'd always found the question of geologists talking about rocks that are so many billions of years old, something completely beyond my comprehension. I can't visualise that depth of time, that depth of experience. Sometimes I look up at the Norman keep which I can see from the garden here and say, 'I'll bet you can tell some stories, sunshine.' Yet that's only going back 900 years. I mean, 900 pounds, 900 pennies, it's nothing, it's something one can assimilate and control in one's mind. It's acceptable. We are a numerate society, and time is very relevant: time is money. Everything has its time base, and when you start to work out those seventy years, how many weeks, days, minutes, it is, it's a number you can comprehend. Suddenly you realise how finite the whole thing is. There's nothing permanent about it.

Most of Cathy's clothes are still in the house. I cleared out some underwear, but I don't know what I'm going to do with the everyday stuff. When a husband leaves home he takes his clothes with him: she was not intending to go away that night. My mother-in-law wanted to do it, and I wanted to do it, so it didn't get done. Also I find that if the nanny moves pieces of furniture I get terribly fidgetty, even angry. It's where I put it, it's where Cathy put it, and whether Cathy is there or not, I'm wasting time, and time is finite. But clothes are so close: people's clothes smell of them and that's incredibly difficult. Recently on a train I smelt the perfume that Cathy always used to wear; smelling the hot, familiar smell, and not knowing where it came from, was not funny. Of all one's senses, smell is probably the most advanced: to me it has the greatest capacity for mental image. One is so discerning about sound. Sight is definitive. Smell is like reading a novel, you can put your own picture to it.

I don't want to replace Cathy as such, but I am a reasonably normal, adult male with two small boys, and I have a practical requirement to be fulfilled. The unpractical side of it is that it has to be dealt with to suit me, it has to be emotionally satisfying as far as I'm concerned, it has to be aesthetically satisfying. It's got to be somebody who sounds right, who smells right, because smell is highly evocative or repulsive. I'm not actually searching at the moment, but I am aware of the fact that I'm going to have to. I know it will be like jumping the jumps second time round – perhaps there's a danger that I know too much, having been married for nine years. But I have so many practical problems to deal with and I am a single parent family: it's been brought home to me very rapidly, inasmuch as I'm now assessed as a bachelor, tax-wise. Isn't that lovely?

My role has changed in so far as it has widened, or been extended: I still have to provide, but I've got new demands on me which leave me no time to identify with *me*. I'm not looking to please somebody else at the moment other than the two children. When I become more adept at dealing with things, I may start looking to please other people. Socially my identity has changed very much because there are a lot of people around who would think twice about asking me to dinner. I've become a bit of a hot number: 'Do we or don't we?', whereas before not a second thought would have been given to inviting us. I'm even paranoid about invitations, and anyway social occasions merely pronounce the difference between me and everyone else. It's a lonely experience. But it hasn't disorientated me; Cathy and I always loved being at home anyway.

I don't feel isolated but in a practical sense I know I am

isolated. I am aware of a certain social stigma but I don't feel it. I expected it, so it didn't come as a shock or a surprise. People, friends and acquaintances, have very little experience to draw on when dealing with me, they don't know what to expect and they don't know how I'm going to react; they're a little frightened. The other evening a bunch of people were round here and one of them said, 'Oh, God, I feel like death.' They looked at me and said, 'Oh, oh, I am sorry.' I said, 'Don't worry, it's a perfectly normal word.' Why should that word cut me to the quick? But all in all, society isn't generous: they don't understand what I'm going through and if they saw me enjoying myself again they wouldn't be sympathetic. They wouldn't say, 'Look, he's had a rotten time; he deserves a break. About time he had a good time.' For a while at least that wouldn't be permissible.

My doctor is a personal friend and I've been able to talk to him a lot. He will not administer heavy tranquillizers without extremely good reason. There was one occasion when things had gone wrong here right from the morning post: I had a tax demand of enormous proportions – I had to pay the probate fees and transfer tax for the boys and I didn't know how I was going to cope. As the day went on I wound up more and more, and by bedtime I knew I wouldn't get a wink's sleep. I gave Don a ring and said, 'Come on round and stick something up my backside just to give me a break.' He resisted and tried to relax me by sharing a bottle of scotch, but he just could not get me drunk, however hard he tried. Alcohol was not going to do the trick, which as I said at the outset goes to show that it doesn't work. In the end he relented and gave me a jab.

Apart from that I've hardly used tranquillizers. The night that Cathy died my father drove me over to see her parents because I was determined to tell them to their faces myself. Maybe it was the wrong decision, but it's the way I've been brought up: you take things square on and there's no ducking it. Apparently I said to the doctor who was sticking an injection into me, 'What are you giving me?' and she said, 'Just something to quieten you down.' I said, 'No, I want to go and tell her parents,' so she gave me only half the dose and left some valium for me. I used that for the cremation and the memorial service. The only other time I used it was when I had to deal with a friend who died in hospital: then a week later I took the damn great jam-jar of the things and flushed them down the loo. In effect they helped no more than booze.

The accident happened at eight o'clock at night and I was kept waiting, hanging around here, until nearly two in the morning for the CID to come. It was hard while it was going on, but I understand that it was right that they had to come, to verify that it was accidental. After it happened I was not so much in a state of shock as in a state of severe exposure. Apparently the local copper when he arrived was not so much concerned about Cathy; he knew what the outcome was there, but he was distinctly of the impression that I was in danger and he was worried that he was going to lose me as well. I had complete hypothermia. I still don't remember a vast chunk of time: I remember things only because people have told me bits and filled in the blanks; but they're still like points down a graph, they're not the line.

I've got plenty to keep me occupied. Two and a half acres of garden has got to be dealt with, and that's creative: I will not let it get behind. Cathy did a lot. It helps to fight off the depression: depression has taken over to the extent of often feeling a complete and absolute falling-in and feeling that there's no way out. Like the time I broke down in the office. Looking back at it rationally, it was an absolutely natural human way of dealing with the problem: let it all hang out, go home and sleep it off. Leading up to that I hadn't slept at all for several nights; I'd been out too late at night because I knew if I went to bed I wouldn't sleep anyway.

I'm restless to the degree that keeping the house tidy has become a fetish. Perhaps it's got something to do with survival and keeping the children well. I'm still very much in love with Cathy and I will be for a long time I think. There's no reason to fight against it, but I do feel that I am able to control the time base on which I'm going to alter things. I don't have to get emotionally involved with other people, male or female, until I'm ready to do so. I don't have to get involved in the finishing of the house – it doesn't look particularly pretty but there's no motivation to get involved; there's no-one to share it with. The kids don't care a damn about things like that, they accept things. I rather hope I'll do things well for them, though, that things will be tidy and well cared for, because I've had great pleasure in a well cared-for life.

Some of the things I think are the hardest are horribly material things, like presents I bought for Cathy. And my wedding ring: now do I take it off or leave it on? I did say to the undertakers, 'Leave Cathy's ring on,' and I now feel I might have worn it next to mine. But some people would say that's ostentatious. Something else that I found difficult was that I had a request from my father-in-law to wear a black tie for a long period of time. I did up until a little while ago, and then I thought, 'Oh, sod it.' So people know you're in mourning and don't crack awful jokes, but they do say I haven't lost my sense of humour. After all, some people adjust very quickly; they can take in the most horrendous situations and adjust in an instant. It varies. An aunt of Cathy's who was widowed when she was fifty said to me, 'You know, you will know when your life is changing because you will find one morning you will wake up and the first thing you will think of is something other than Cathy.' With two little bounders like that it may not take so long.

The children have taken it without a problem. Not one. We talk about her. In this household we have always had prayers as we go to sleep each night, and we had, 'God bless Grannies and Grandpas, God bless Daddy, God bless Nanny, God bless everything under the sun.' And lately, 'Ask Jesus to look after Mummy.' That, funnily enough, was their answer, not mine. Edward, who is four, has got over it much more quickly inasmuch as if I didn't say it one night, he would still be quite happy. Paul, who is five, would be terribly upset if we didn't say 'God bless Mummy and ask Jesus to look after Mummy,' and when he's said it he always finishes it by saying, 'Dear Mummy.' And it's no better any night. Dear little chap. And yet it's a great comfort. Oh for the simplicity of a child's mind: they are a comfort. One night Paul was obviously hot or cold or wanted a pee or something and he couldn't get back to sleep. He said, 'I want to come into your bed, Daddy,' so finally I said, 'OK, come on,' and he came through and settled in and he went straight to sleep. Suddenly I found I was fast asleep too: I was so used to having someone else sleeping beside me.

I was actually very lucky with them. My mother was here the next day and I didn't know what was going on really. I was sitting on the hearth in front of the fire and what took place was almost like one of those Pooh Bear scenes. The two boys were sitting on the carpet by my knee and Paul said 'Where's Mummy?' Fortunately the right words, in the right order, came, and I was able to say 'Mummy has gone to Jesus.' They do have some experience of it in their own way because Great Grandpa died and one or two other people they knew as well. 'Oh,' said Paul, 'Did she go in a car?' So I said, 'Not exactly.' Then he changed his tack and said, 'What happened?' I said, 'Well, you know I told you about the pond and how you mustn't play near it? Last night Mummy fell through the ice and went under the water.' 'Oh,' he said, 'silly Mummy.' Edward didn't say a thing; he just listened and took it all in. Paul was asking the questions and Edward was listening to all the answers.

I've had it in the neck from Paul several times since then – he has become a little obsessed with the mechanics of what happened. 'What was Mummy wearing?' So I said, 'Her sheepskin jacket.' 'What skirt was she wearing? What jumper was she wearing?' So I told him. 'Was she wearing her blue pants or her white pants?' At that point I had to say, 'Paul, I don't know.' I suppose he wants to know the details so it makes it real to him; perhaps that's his way of coming to terms with it and accepting it. You can't read a child's mind. Anyway it's been for these past four months an absolutely golden rule that every question he asks, or that either of them asks, gets an absolutely straight answer. There's no fudging it, there's no hedging around it. I had a pretty rough one from Paul the other day: 'When can we have a new Mummy, Daddy?'

But the chain is broken. There are many ways of breaking

the chain – it can be death or separation or divorce. But oh God I hate being on my own. The children help, music helps, and there's my dog – they all start to bridge the gap. And my family have been marvellous; my old nanny came in the next day and stayed for a fortnight until the new nanny arrived. She was super; she dealt with all kinds of problems like me falling asleep on the sofa at three in the morning with the headphones on – that sort of thing. I'm very lucky with my family; not unique with it though. I've still got a super relationship with my parents, it couldn't be better.

A kind of unconventional religion has helped me too. I am a Christian and I sometimes believe in the hereafter, that it's a much better place and so forth. I have a developing feeling in fact that what we refer to as Heaven and Hell are not places or things, they are nothing other than what our memory is in the eyes of those people left behind. Time will undoubtedly help too. I accept the fact that she isn't there: it's very practical, she isn't. The changes are many, inasmuch as there are many many things that we would have discussed and done together, and sorted out together; and now they have to be done *tout seul*. But you can't do anything else but accept it when you've actually seen somebody die. You can't do anything else. You have to accept that there's been a change: one minute somebody's there, and the next minute they're not.

Seeing somebody die isn't either shocking or harrowing: I saw my grandmother die, I was with her when she died. We were keeping vigils as a family round the clock. And I saw a guy killed in a car crash. Cathy was obviously the most important one. I don't find the situation, the fact of death, frightening. I don't find it disquieting. My grandmother was breathing one minute and not the next. The same applied to the lad in the car, exactly the same. I've not seen in any of those situations a fear of death; I've not heard of anybody that has really been afraid of dying when it came to it. People who know they're dying are less nervous about it than the people who know that they know they're dying. They are absolutely calm, no sweat, no panic. I don't worry about my own death, I'm not frightened of it.

I wonder how much I am suffering: I suppose I will realise afterwards actually. A hell of a lot, is the answer. I suppose there's a lot of natural anaesthesia that goes on while you're suffering. But it's not that bad: I've got the kids, my family, the house, my work. The children have helped me above all else. Number one. They are the reason for carrying on. My parents too, and my brother, have been absolutely fantastic. Friends have been apprehensive about what to do; yet it's great if somebody phones just to say, 'How are you?', because I know that they are thinking of me. This place helps too: Cathy and I took this place from a jungle and I ain't going to let it go back to a jungle. I've had about 101 people tell me to move, and I've said to 103 of them, 'Get lost. You don't know what you're talking about.' What am I frightened of? The place isn't haunted. It's a part of me and a perfectly normal, natural family house. It happens to be occupied at the moment by a one-parent family, but it is still a family.

I must admit that I do find cutting the grass past the place where Cathy fell in very difficult. Basically I don't understand it, it just doesn't seem logical. Yet looking over the pond from here, I sometimes find it quite comforting actually. I sometimes think she's still in there – the part of her that matters is still there. Her special places are a comfort too. We both had our own desks. I never use mine now, I use hers. I feel very at ease sitting there and dealing with all the nasty mundania of life – writing the bloody gas bill and the tax bill and the rates bill. I feel in myself, whereas I haven't got it licked, I've been able to organise it, luckily, into sort of little boxes. Not to rationalise what's happened, but to analyse my thoughts and more or less to accept the situation. Not to keep turning back and saying, 'If only, if only'. However much we bitch and whine, we can't change it.

16

HELEN:
gay bereavement

Helen and Madeleine were lovers for twenty-five years, not living together but spending long periods in each others' company. When they met, Helen was married with two children and, although her husband never acknowledged it, her children came to accept the relationship and the fact of their mother's lesbianism. Madeleine's family, on the other hand, never knew her secret, never met Helen and never suspected that she was gay. Nor did her employers know, and Madeleine went to great lengths to guard her secret.

When they first met in the 1960s, homosexuality was only just out of the realms of illegality, and frequently aroused vitriolic feelings in many people. In a more tolerant climate a quarter of a century later, Helen, now in her sixties, felt that it was important – in spite of the evident pain that it caused her – to air the special problems faced by gay people in situations of death and bereavement. Their intention, she told me, was that when they both retired they would finally live together. It was not to be. Madeleine died thirteen years ago.

If we want to get at the kernel, we must break the shell.

Meister Eckhart (1260–1327)

Madeleine was going to spend Christmas with her family. She loved working with leather, and was making me a beautiful leather photo album as a Christmas present. We had spent hours rifling through shoe boxes and envelopes for the most elusive pictures of the past twenty-five years – even the ghastliest were included. I remember our amusement looking at those candid camera shots. She took it with her to work on, knowing that she would have time on her hands.

She left London two days before Christmas, promising to phone. Our arrangement had always been that when she visited her family, who didn't know of our relationship, that she would ring me, and I went along with that. But there was no phone call, not even on Christmas Day. I could endure the silence no longer. I decided to phone her. I asked to speak to Madeleine and the reply was, 'She's dead.' Down went the receiver.

I rang again, and different voices, hostile, nasty, abusive, refused to give me any real information. Eventually a woman who identified herself as the niece told me with venom in her voice that Madeleine had had a heart attack. She employed a special brand of abuse and calculated cruelty which has the power to wound deeply. She told me, gleefully, that I was to blame.

They had found the photographs and destroyed them. Every one. The times that I have been asked, since, for photographs of her – and I have nothing. This is something which suddenly caught up with me later. The family gave me wrong information about the funeral and ended up saying, 'We don't want you there, you have nothing to do with her.' I was not allowed to go to Madeleine's funeral; no question. I have no idea where her grave is, although I tried to find out. I have a feeling she was probably cremated and that there is no grave. It was very, very cruel, their whole attitude.

It was a particularly cold winter and the only telephone we have is out in the hall, where it was freezing. I was just sitting there. It was quite horrendous. Their obstructiveness was really cruel – there was a lot of calculated cruelty from members of the family.

She had a small flat in Notting Hill Gate, where I kept a lot of my things. It wasn't the first thing on my mind to go and collect them; by the time I got up there it had been stripped bare. There was nothing, absolutely nothing. I walked in there, expecting to see it how it had been: it never,

never occurred to me. We tried to keep everything of ours in the flat – it was our safe haven. That was a real trauma. It was like going into a tomb. Complete emptiness. That really hit me, it really brought it home to me. So I have nothing of hers – except for a necklace she bought, and a few little knick-knacks.

I realised that in order to retain my own self-respect, I would not pursue the family any further. I don't know whether they kept my things aside for me or not, but I thought, 'No, I won't do this.' I had missed the funeral, and if they considered that 'winning', I wasn't going to make them feel still better about making me squirm. They were very, very unpleasant over the phone – all the negative things you can say about homosexuals: terms like 'corruption' and God knows what. I shut off after a time, and thought to myself, 'sticks and stones ...' But on top of everything else it was really, really hard.

Bereavement is a weird state to be in. At first I was numb: I really didn't take it in that she had died. I would walk into a room thinking that she would still be there. It was quite a shock that she wasn't. It was getting used to that that was so hard. There wasn't any bereavement counselling around to speak of, and it was really difficult to talk to people about it. I had one particular friend to whom I could talk, who would listen, who knew her well, who liked her, and that was good.

I clutched at straws. I was listening to a radio programme one day and they started talking about visualisation. I thought, 'That sounds a jolly good idea.' So I started doing visualisation and it was fantastic. I visualised her sitting next to me, and I could see her. You see, I had not said goodbye. That was the hardest bit. When people go away for a short time it's not a big deal. By visualising her – and I can still do it today, when I go out somewhere and it is particularly beautiful – I find myself talking to her. It's not morbid, it's just a feeling that I would like to share this pleasant thing with her. That was a tremendous help, because I could say all the things I hadn't said.

We *don't* tell people we love them while they are alive. We can be pretty harsh and negative, fault-finding and nitpicking, no matter how fond we are of somebody. It's always the faults that are enlarged! I was suddenly able to reverse that, and that was a tremendous relief.

I don't honestly know how long this bereavement process lasts, or how (or whether) it all comes together. At present I am working at the Terence Higgins Trust with young people who have AIDS. After the last funeral I went to I was absolutely devastated – out of total proportion to my feelings towards the person who had died. I was very fond of them, we had worked together and been out for dinners, but we weren't bosom friends. It took me five or six weeks to recover from going to that funeral. I just couldn't understand why I should feel so devastated. But recently I realised that my problem around going to funerals was that I didn't go to Madeleine's. You wouldn't think that after all this time – thirteen years – that was still stored up inside. Not only did I not go to Madeleine's, I didn't go to my mother's either.

These things do not go away of their own accord. It is amazing how you suddenly realise, 'This is the reason why I behaved like that.' Our inner emotions, those of which we are not even aware, can colour our whole outlook. We are carrying them around, and until we are aware of them, they get projected on to other people.

I feel that bereavement is an ongoing thing. It is not that one becomes morbid, it is that, up to a point, our grief is their memorial. It keeps them alive – they live through our memories of them. I think that is important. The bad things disappear, and that is nice. One looks at one's past through rosy-tinted spectacles. All the campaigning that we did – CND marches, Vietnam marches, whatever – sometimes they were tedious and we'd row, but in retrospect weren't they good times!

Sometimes when I am low, I can't cope with the retelling. I feel that I am devaluing my own experiences. But I do understand the value of people understanding about the time factor, how time does help to heal, and also the importance of understanding about the frustration and anger. And there is a lot of anger. She died! The frustration! Why? Why did she do this? How could she leave me behind? We didn't finish off what we were doing. I was left here with such anger. And on the other hand, there was this feeling of, 'Oh God! She was on her own.' The conflict of emotions devastated me.

In the beginning I became withdrawn and I was a zombie. I am not keen on taking pills but I actually took a couple of tranquillizers in spite of being very anti-drugs. Something had happened that I just could not understand. These various emotions were fighting inside me and I was absolutely helpless, there was nothing I could do.

Working with AIDS as I do now, I find that lots of lovers' parents, brothers, sisters, will refuse for the life-support machines to be turned off, because they can't let go. In a way I can understand that. If I had been there with Madeleine, even if I had known that she would have been brain damaged, I would have wanted to resuscitate her – because *I* needed her. This is the problem: her needs against mine. From that point of view, we are selfish, in being unable to let go.

Until we learn to let go, the bereavement is traumatic. It will bring up all the negative things. As soon as you can let go, then it becomes quite beautiful. Bereavement then is – I wouldn't say a pleasure – but it fits into your lifestyle ... of sharing. It's not heart-rending all the time: it can even be a good feeling. That doesn't mean to say that when you hear a certain tune, you don't suddenly go, 'Wow, I wish she was here.' That is overwhelming.

How to let go of anger? Personally, I threw myself into gay politics. When Madeleine died I realised that I must do something. I had been a nominal member of CHE, the Campaign for Homosexual Equality. She had had to be very careful, she was frightened for her job and her parents finding out, and I respected that. But now I joined a local group, and they were lovely, lovely people. Although they didn't realise it, they helped me enormously. They made me campaign secretary and that meant writing to MPs, and I had a whale of a time. That is what took over. The anger was therefore diffused: I could use it against people who were homophobic, so that it dissolved away. That was really good, because otherwise I would have dumped it around indiscriminately.

My daughter was very supportive, and so were some marvellous friends. Without them I don't know what I would have done. You suddenly realise how very important friends are. But even going to work, where they knew about Madeleine and I, they thought, 'Well, she was just a friend.' They didn't understand that I could possibly grieve. That was very hard. There was never any contact again with her family, and no support at all from my husband. He is into total denial as far as anything to do with me is concerned. Our relationship broke up in 1950, we have lived our own lives for forty years, but he lives in an ostrich world, he buries his head regarding anything he considers unpleasant.

There was quite a funny reaction from gay friends, women who were in relationships. Was I going to be a predator? I never looked on myself as a predator. Perhaps it is a problem with all relationships – but I suppose you are more aware of it in gay ones: the fragility of them, sometimes, because there aren't so many of us who are recognisable, and poaching does happen. I suppose there is this feeling of insecurity.

One thing that I am very aware of since she died is that I am definitely incapable of making further relationships – and not for any sentimental reason. This is the schizophrenia of one's emotions. You are suddenly free, and there is a degree of freedom which is very liberating. You can go where you want, you don't have to account for your movements, you don't have to account for anything. But then you suddenly feel guilty, because your sorrow can be tinged with some delight. We are very good at feeling guilty. But this is only part of the story: it has to be weighed up against the huge loss of somebody close to you.

All these emotions come to the fore, and we have never been taught how to deal with emotions. While Madeleine was alive I was always interested in psychology, and in the '60s you could go to Gestalt and all kinds of other therapies. We had a really good time going round them all. Things rub off, you begin to understand something about yourself by examining your own emotions. I also did a residential marriage guidance course, and again you have to look at yourself because you need to relate to other people. All these counselling training courses certainly helped me enormously to understand myself and what was going on. Not to be frightened to cry when I really wanted to, or to bang my head against a wall, or beat a pillow.

My biggest therapy was – and still is today – going to Speakers' Corner at Marble Arch, getting on the platform and speaking. It is tremendously good therapy. I don't care whether people listen or not, but it is something I get out of my system. It is a legitimate place where you have permission to do those sorts of things – and we seem to need permission.

You still hear of gay people today who live together, and who fail to make a will. The partner is turfed out of the home – a home that often he or she has helped to pay for. There is no common-law-husband/wife law that protects them. So the family takes over, and the partner has no rights in law at all. It is quite horrendous. The times that you hear of somebody who has nursed their lover with AIDS, after living with them for years, and somehow it never occurred to them that the other guy would be turfed out on to the streets with nothing. What can you prove if the flat is in another person's name? The law will not protect you. The message is, you have to make a watertight will. Yet the number of families who nonetheless will put a caveat on the will – anything to delay things. It is still happening to this day. It is a tragedy that society doesn't want to learn, and that it even wants to inflict pain on people in my situation.

I was brought up a Roman Catholic but I am a good atheist. I look at this world and I can't have a faith. It would take a warped mind to create human beings, and I can't see an all-loving entity having a warped mind. I adore going into churches, I love the smell of incense. I enjoy listening to church services, basically for the music, and the atmosphere of the church. I can understand that it enhances your spirituality, but you can forget about a deity.

None of that was changed by Madeleine's death. I had given up after Germany: only a warped deity could ever condone anything like what I saw there as a child. I lost my parents in horrendous circumstances. My father was murdered in a Nazi concentration camp when I was thirteen, and my mother died in an extermination camp. I heard about her death when I was twenty-one, here in England. In those days I was nursing, and I saw many young people die of tuberculosis, for which there wasn't a cure. So my experience of death had always been violent of sorts.

I came out of Germany in 1939, just before the war started. I was sixteen then; old enough to know what was going on. I came from a very aware family – my father was a well-known Social Democrat who was beaten to death in 1936 because of his political attitude against Nazism. He had gone around denouncing Hitler, and telling people what was going on in the Spanish Civil War. So they locked him up.

I heard of his death over the radio. I happened to be at home alone, because my mother was out with my aunt – we had moved in with them in Hanover. When she came in I thought, I can't possibly tell her. I was thirteen years old. I have three brothers, the youngest of whom is fifteen years older than I.

I grieved for him intensely. One of my brothers realised that I couldn't cope with anybody saying anything to me. He told me, 'You have to learn to just smile at them, and they won't say anything.' I could not, at that time, take anybody expressing any condolences. I took myself off to museums, art galleries, symphony concerts – whatever happened to be on. I couldn't stay in at home. I wandered. People at that time were allowed to collect the coffin from the concentration camp, and so I went to the funeral. It was a cremation, and I can still hear the cranking of the coffin. Those memories are alive.

At the time there was so much horror going on that I was pushed out of Germany. I had to leave my family behind, which is a bereavement in itself: it is another kind of bereavement, which has haunted me for years. My mother took me to the station in Hanover and when the train pulled out – so many refugees have said exactly the same – the figure became smaller and smaller. She was later taken to an extermination camp, so there was no funeral for her. For years, I would see a woman walking in front of me, and the outline would bring back that memory: and I would run up to her. It took years to heal, seeing people I thought might be her – until I knew she was dead and then I realised it couldn't be her.

I was nursing in a hospital, and I remember matron sending for me. A letter had come from the Red Cross, and she knew that somebody should be around when I opened it. That was the sort of bereavement I had learned to deal with. I also realised that for my own mental health to survive I had to stay away from other refugees. It was very comforting in the beginning just to talk about things at home, but I soon realised that if I did that I would never move forwards. So I made a conscious decision that I would try to forget everything German. I changed my name, which gave me a new identity. This was very important to me as part of the healing process.

Anger and bitterness are very destructive – to oneself as well as to others, because you take the anger out on people around you. I was lucky in that I had enough enlightened friends around me to help me with this. Going into politics got my anger out, too. I could dissipate my anger that way, by getting my message across. So it became something positive, that I was using up the anger within me. The destructive part, in bereavement, is when we use anger against each other. I am very worried that so few counselling agencies are employed for areas like this. That is how families can break up, and they often don't understand what has broken them up. It is because they are using the anger against each other. People do not understand the nature of anger. They blame. But you can actually talk this out – if you talk, it melts away. But very few people can – they choose confrontation.

But it takes two. You may have one person who is ready to talk, but the other is like a brick wall, and completely resists. So – total destruction of relationship. You look back in your life and you think, how sad. Why does this person need this brick wall? He will react like this for the rest of his life, without understanding what is going on for himself. That is the destructive part of anger.

I have been to quite a few gay bereavement counselling sessions and found them very helpful – although some counsellors understand the problems better than others. There are variations of bereavement and I think we should make greater use of *loss*: whether it is losing your job, or the loss of a friend when people split up, or death. The bitterness, anger, and all the expectations around it – it's all a form of bereavement. Yet we should look at the positive side: I am alive, I have my freedom, I have my memories and these are very helpful. I can look back and smile. I can still visualise and share – that is important.

The freedom, of course, has a negative side. I go somewhere alone, I come back alone, and that can be quite devastating. There is a positive and negative side to everything. I am sixty-seven now, and it is my choice to be free – so it probably will be to the end of my days. It is a pattern I have grown into. I don't mind being alone. I am very rarely aware of being *lonely* – that is different. I have a lot of acquaintances, but only two really very close friends, and my daughter. We have a good understanding; we share without treading on each other's toes.

I have learnt through all my years, and through working with people with AIDS, how fragile life is. That you should do things for yourself, and not pretend that you are doing things for other people. Be honest with yourself about it. Why *should* people have to appreciate what you do? It is important to love yourself. Time catches up with us: the years fly by and it makes you look at things, especially when working with AIDS: these people may not have any future time. It makes me live in the present. I couldn't care less whether people think I am smartly dressed or whether I am beautiful or ugly – those things become meaningless. It makes living with yourself so much more comfortable. I wish I had learned it much earlier in life.

WHERE TO GO FOR HELP

Cruse
126 Sheen Road
Richmond
Surrey TW9 1UR
Tel: 081 940 4818

Cruse branches offer help and counselling to all bereaved people who live in their area. Regular social meetings offer an opportunity for contact between bereaved people. Cruse fact sheets and an extensive booklist are obtainable through your local branch or from Cruse headquarters.

Foundation for the Study of Infant Deaths (Cot Death Research and Support)
35 Belgrave Square
London SW1X 8QB
Tel: 071 235 0965
Cot death helpline: 071 235 1721

Support and help for parents with a cot death bereavement.

SANDS (Stillbirth and neo-natal death society)
28 Portland Place
London WIN 4DE
Tel: 071 436 5881

A self-help organisation offering understanding and encouragement to parents bereaved by stillbirth, and newborn babies.

Miscarriage Association
PO Box 24
Ossett
West Yorkshire WF5 9XG
Tel: 0924 830515

Offers information and support for women and their families, with support groups nationwide.

SATFA (Support after Termination for Abnormality)
29-30 Soho Square
London WIV 6JB
Tel: 071 439 6124

Support for people who have lost one twin
Karran Youngs
54 Park Way
Exeter
Devon EX2 9NP
Tel: 0392 431605

Support for people who have lost both twins
Sue Manning
32 Denton Court Road
Gravesend
Kent
Tel: 0474 567320

Bereaved Parents' Helpline
6 Canon's Gate
Harlow
Essex
Tel: 0279 412745/39685

A group which works locally in the Harlow area, but which is happy to talk to parents anywhere and refer them if necessary.

The Compassionate Friends
6 Denmark Street
Bristol BS1 5DQ
Tel: 0272 292778

A nationwide self-help organisation for bereaved parents whose child of any age, including adult, has died from any cause, including murder. They offer friendship and understanding, as opposed to counselling; personal and group support; plus a quarterly newsletter, a postal library and a wide range of leaflets. Compassionate Friends has numerous branches and area representatives.

Relaxation for Living
29 Burwood Park Road
Walton-on-Thames
Surrey KT12 5LH

A group offering a practical and holistic approach to stress management, which has produced a booklet called 'Easing Grief' (35p incl. p and p).

The Samaritans
17 Uxbridge Road
Slough
Berkshire
Tel: 0753 32713

A nationwide network answering distress calls and offering a listening ear. Look in your local phone directory for your area number.

National Association of Widows
54-57 Allison Street
Digbeth
Birmingham B5 5TH
Tel: 021 643 8348

Offers help and friendship to widows. Local branches nationwide.

Age Concern
England
Astral House
126-128 London Road
London SW16 4EJ
Tel: 081 679 8000

Scotland
54a Fountainbridge
Edinburgh EH3 9PT
Tel: 031 228 5656

Wales
4th Floor
1 Cathedral Road
Cardiff
S. Glamorgan
Tel: 0222 371 566

Northern Ireland
6 Lower Crescent
Belfast BT7 1NR
Tel: 0232 245729

Offers bereavement counselling in some areas, and can give much general support to the elderly. They have a wide range of fact sheets on practical problems facing the elderly, especially housing.

Gay Bereavement Project
Unitarian Rooms
Hoop Lane
London NW11 8BS
Tel: 081 455 8894

Foundation for Black Bereaved Families
Lorrene Hunt
11 Kingston Square
Salters Hill
London SE19
Tel: 081 761 7228

Hospice Information Service
St Christopher's Hospice
51-59 Lawrie Park Road
Sydenham
London SE26 6DZ
Tel: 081 778 9252

Carers' Association
29 Chilworth Mews
London W2 3RG
Tel: 071 724 7776

Has groups nationwide which provide support for people looking after other people who cannot manage without help. They offer a bereavement service to carers after the death of the person they were caring for.

Cancerlink
17 Britannia Street
London WC1X 8JN
Tel: 071 833 2451

London Association of Bereavement Services
68 Charlton Street
London NW1 1JR
Tel: 071 388 2153

Acts as a co-ordinating body for small community-based bereavement services throughout London.

Bibliography

BOOKS

J. Agee, *A Death in the Family*. London: Peter Owen, 1971 (Panther edn, 1973).

Helen Alexander (ed), *Living with Dying*. London: BBC Publications, 1990.

Mog Ball, *Death*. Oxford University Press (Standpoints series), 1976.

Simone de Beauvoir, *A Very Easy Death*. Harmondsworth: Penguin Books, 1969.

John Bowlby, *Attachment and Loss* (2 vols). Harmondsworth: Penguin Books, 1973.

Lindy Burton, *Care of the Child facing Death*. London: Routledge & Kegan Paul, 1974.

Lynne Caine, *Widow*. New York: Bantam Books, 1975.

Elizabeth Collick, *Through Grief: the bereavement journey*. London: Dartman, Longman and Todd/Cruse, 1986.

Mary Craig, *Blessings*. London: Hodder & Stoughton (Coronet edn), 1979.

E. Furman, *A Child's Parent Dies: Studies in Childhood Bereavement*. Yale University Press, 1974.

Susan Hill, *In the Springtime of the Year*. London: Hamish Hamilton, 1974 (Penguin edn, 1977).

John Hinton, *Dying*. Harmondsworth: Penguin Books (Pelican edn), 1969.

Elisabeth Kübler-Ross, *On Death and Dying*. London: Tavistock Publications, 1970.

Elisabeth Kübler-Ross, *To Live Until We Say Goodbye*. New York: Prentice-Hall, 1979.

C. S. Lewis, *A Grief Observed*. London: Faber, 1964.

P. Marris, *Widows and their Families*. London: Routledge & Kegan Paul, 1958.

P. Marris, *Loss and Change*. London: Routledge & Kegan Paul, 1974.

Raymond A. Moody, *Life After Life*. London: Transworld (Corgi edn), 1975.

Murray Parkes, Colin, *Bereavement: Studies of Grief in Adult Life*. London: Tavistock Publications, 1972 (Pelican revised edn, 1986).

M. Pelgrin, *And a Time to Die*. London: Routledge & Kegan Paul, 1961.

L. Pinkus, *Death and the Family*. London: Faber, 1976.

Michael Rutter, *Children of Sick Parents*. Oxford University Press, 1966.

Michael Rutter, *Maternal Deprivation Reassessed*. Harmondsworth: Penguin Books, 1972.

H. Sarnoff Schiff, *The Bereaved Parent*. London: Souvenir Press, 1977.

S. Stephens, *Death Comes Home*. London: Mowbray, 1972.

Judy Tatelbaum, *The Courage to Grieve*. London: Heinemann, 1981.

Margaret Torrie, *Begin Again*. London: Dent, 1975.

A. Toynbee, *Man's Concern with Death*. New York: McGraw-Hill, 1969.

Rosemary Wells, *Helping Children Cope with Grief*. London: Sheldon Press, 1988.

S. Wolff, *Children Under Stress*. London: Allen Lane, 1969 (Penguin edn, 1973).

PAPERS AND ARTICLES

J. Birtchell, Psychiatric breakdown following recent parental death, *Brit. J. Med. Psychol.*, 48 (1975), p. 379.

D. Black, What happens to bereaved children? *Proc. Roy. Soc. Med.*, 69, 11 (1976), p. 842.

J. Bowlby, Processes of mourning, *Int. J. Psychoanal.*, 42 (1961), p. 317.

H. Jolly, Family reactions to stillbirth, *Proc. Roy. Soc. Med.*, 69 (1976), p. 837.

G. P. Kooker, Talking with children about death, *Amer. J. Orthopsych.*, 44 (1974), p. 404.

E. Lewis, The management of stillbirth, *Lancet*, 48 (1975), p. 379.

E. Lewis, The abhorrence of stillbirth, *Lancet*, June 4 (1977), leading article.

E. Lewis, Mourning by the family after a stillbirth or neonatal death, *Archives of Disease in Childhood*, 54 (1979), p. 303.

E. Lewis with Anne Page, Failure to mourn a stillbirth, *Brit. J. Med. Psychol.*, 51 (1978), p. 237.

Lady Limerick, Support and counselling needs of families following a cot death bereavement, *Proc. Roy. Soc. Med.*, 69 (1976), p. 839.

S. Lindemann, The symptomatology and management of acute grief, *Amer. J. Psychiat.*, (1944).

D. Morris, Parent reaction to peri-natal death. *Proc. Roy. Soc. Med.*, 69 (1976), p. 837.

C. Murray Parkes, Determinants of outcome following bereavement, *Omega*, 6 (1976), p. 303.

C. Reeves, Treatment of children following the death of a parent, *J. Ment. Sci.*, 107 (1961), p. 754.

C. Saunders, The management of terminal illness, *Hospital Medicine* (Dec. 1966).

S. E. Schowalter, How do children and funerals mix? *Journal of Paediatrics*, 1 (1976), p. 139.

D. M. Shepherd and B. M. Barraclough, The aftermath of parental suicide for children, *Brit. J. Psychiat.*, 129 (1976), p. 267.

'What to do when someone dies', Consumers Association Publication.

'What to do after a death' free DHSS leaflet no D49.

There is special providence in the fall of a sparrow. If it be now, 'tis not to come – if it be not to come, it will be now – if it be not now, yet it will come – the readiness is all.

Shakespeare: *Hamlet*

More books from Optima

A SAFER PLACE TO CRY by Dr Brian Roet

Under stress? Lacking confidence? Feeling depressed?

During therapy, many people burst into tears as if they have found the only safe place to cry and come to terms with problems that disturb their peace of mind and undermine their physical health.

In his new book, Dr Brian Roet – best-selling author of *All In The Mind?* – shows us how we can use therapeutic techniques to release deep-seated emotions, acknowledge our strengths and weaknesses, and establish emotional equilibrium. Drawing upon numerous case histories and years of professional experience, his reassuring and practical advice guides us towards new ways to enjoy a more fulfilling life.

ISBN 0 356 17603 7
Price (in UK only) **£5.99**

**DO-IT-YOURSELF PSYCHOTHERAPY by Dr Martin
Shepard**

- Would you like to understand yourself better?
- Do you want to lead a richer, more fulfilled life?

Dr Martin Shepard draws on his long experience as a professional
therapist to present this 'do-it-yourself' approach that provides a
real alternative to formal psychotherapy. Each chapter focuses on
one aspect of human behaviour and concludes with a series of
exercises designed to give you a clearer understanding of your own
thoughts and responses.

    This book is extremely practical, helpful and easy to follow. It
will not only enhance your enjoyment of life, but save you a for-
tune in therapist's fees.

ISBN 0 356 15413 0
Price (in UK only) **£4.95**

THE MENTAL HEALTH SURVIVAL GUIDE by Elaine Farrell

- 1 in 4 people will experience some form of mental distress
- 1 in 10 experience clinical depression some time during their lives
- the main reason for seeing a family doctor is emotional rather than physical
- an estimated 2% of over fifteen-year-olds have significant problems with alcohol dependence

With statistics like these it is obvious that mental distress is a fact of life for many. And whether it is depression, anxiety, phobias, psychosomatic symptoms, alcohol misuse or difficulty in coping with day-to-day life, the problems are there and help is needed.

In this self-help guide, Elaine Farrell dispels the fear and uncertainty surrounding mental distress by providing information on restoring and maintaining good mental health. She covers the many different therapies, drug treatments and alternatives, self-help measures including physical exercise and stress reduction techniques, plus practical advice on finding the right care for you, and understanding your rights. Fully comprehensive, sympathetic and well-presented information makes this book particularly valuable to anyone seeking help for themselves or someone they know.

ISBN 0 356 14021 0
Price (in UK only) **£6.99**

YOUR CANCER, YOUR LIFE by Dr Trish Reynolds

- What is cancer?
- What are the symptoms?
- How can cancer be treated?
- What do chemotherapy, surgery, radiotherapy, hormone treatment involve?
- Do certain treatments cause side effects?
- What does having cancer mean?

Taking a sympathetic but positive approach, Dr Trish Reynolds, a cancer specialist with 10 years' experience, provides the comprehensive information needed by every cancer patient. She explains the different forms and symptoms of cancer, and examines treatments such as surgery, radiotherapy and chemotherapy, balancing their benefits against possible side effects.

With this knowledge, Dr Reynolds encourages you to have the confidence to make positive choices and participate in managing your treatment. Rather than handing over control to the 'experts', she emphasises that *you* are the best judge of what's right for *you*: it's your cancer and your life.

ISBN 0 356 15417 3
Price (in UK only) **£6.95**

THE HOSPICE WAY by Denise Winn

- What are hospices?
- What do they do?
- Where can I find one?
- What do they cost?

Drawing on her own personal experience of nursing her mother who was dying of cancer, Denise Winn here offers a sensitive introduction to the growing hospice movement, and its philosophy of care for the terminally ill.

Hospices provide a very real, sympathetic and increasingly available alternative to hospitals for those who are dying. Denise Winn describes the special skills they have to offer, which include meeting the emotional needs of patients and their relatives, symptom control, bereavement counselling, and the support of the family.

Many hospices also organize home care support teams, and the book provides practical guidance on how to seek hospice help and find further information.

ISBN 0 356 12741 9
Price (in UK only) £3.95

A MATTER OF LIFE by Dr Nadya Coates and Norman Jollyman

The Springhill Centre is a rehabilitation, respite and terminal care centre with a revolutionary approach to the treatment of degenerative and disabling illnesses, including cancer, leukaemia, AIDS, cerebral palsy, spina bifida, multiple sclerosis and strokes.

Emphasising the responsibility of patients for their own health and quality of life, *A Matter of Life* presents the self-help philosophy of Springhill as it outlines ways of improving your health through diet and nutrition, exercise, detoxification, pain control, stress management, relaxation and visualisation. Integrating orthodox medical treatments with a variety of complementary therapies, its affirmative approach offers renewed aspirations, wider horizons and new possibilities for healthcare for people with serious or life-threatening illnesses.

ISBN 0 356 19107 9
Price (in UK only) **£6.99**

DIVORCE AND AFTER: A FATHER'S TALE by Mary
McCormack

- One marriage in three ends in divorce.
- One man in ten gets sole care of his children.
- Fifty per cent of non-custodial parents lose contact with their children after a couple of years.

Much has been said and written about the effects of divorce on mothers and children, but what about fathers? What sort of a deal do fathers get, and what is the impact of divorce on their relationship with their children?

In these telling interviews with men from all backgrounds and circumstances, Mary McCormack traces the experiences and feelings of men from the break-up of their relationship, through the minefield of the legal system, to the rebuilding of their lives. A wealth of experience and advice from numerous professionals, pressure groups and voluntary agencies is also incorporated into this sympathetic and often enlightening book.

ISBN 0 356 17525 1
Price (in UK only) **£5.99**

IMMUNE POWER by Jennifer Meek

The immune system has an amazing capacity to fight illness and disease, but its inefficiency or breakdown can have serious consequences for our health and is related to a variety of conditions, from lacking energy to ME, from recurrent colds to cancer.

This guide shows how you can strengthen and enhance your immune system and with a positive attitude enjoy a healthy, active and long life. Written by a qualified nutritional counsellor, it identifies particular diseases and illnesses and covers topics such as diet and nutrition, vitamins and minerals, exercise and sleep, stress and depression, and the environment and pollution.

ISBN 0 356 17138 8
Price (in UK only) **£5.99**

All Optima books are available at your bookshop or news-agent, or can be ordered from the following address:

Optima Books
Cash Sales Department
PO Box 11
Falmouth
Cornwall TR10 9EN

Alternatively you may fax your order to the above address. Fax number: 0326 76423

Payments can be made as follows: Cheque, postal order (payable to Macdonald & Co (Publishers) Ltd) or by credit cards, Visa/Access. *Do not send cash or currency.*

UK customers, please send a cheque or postal order (no currency) and allow 80p for postage and packing for the first book plus 20p for each additional book up to a maximum charge of £2.00.

BFPO customers, please allow 80p for the first book plus 20p for each additional book.

Overseas customers, including Ireland, please allow £1.50 for postage and packing for the first book, £1.00 for the second book and 30p for each additional book.

NAME (Block letters) ....

ADDRESS ....

....

I enclose my remittance for _____

I wish to pay by Access/Visa Card

Number ☐☐☐☐☐☐☐☐☐☐☐☐☐☐☐☐☐☐

Card expiry date